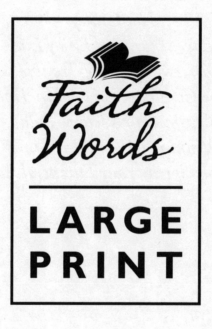

Books by Dr. Creflo Dollar

In the Presence of God
Live Without Fear
Not Guilty
Love, Live, and Enjoy Life
Breaking Out of Trouble
Walking in the Confidence of God in Troubled Times
Claim Your Victory Today
Winning in Troubled Times
The Holy Spirit, Your Financial Advisor

REAL MANHOOD

Being the Man
God Made You to Be

DR. CREFLO DOLLAR

Faith Words

LARGE PRINT

NEW YORK   BOSTON   NASHVILLE

Unless otherwise indicated, all Scripture quotations are from the King James Version of the Holy Bible.

Scripture quotations taken from the Amplified® Bible (AMP), copyright © 1954, 1958, 1962, 1964, 1965, 1987 by The Lockman Foundation. Used by permission (www.Lockman.org).

Scripture quotations marked NLT are taken from the Holy Bible, New Living Translation, copyright © 1996, 2004, 2007 by Tyndale House Foundation. Used by permission of Tyndale House Publishers, Inc., Carol Stream, Illinois 60188. All rights reserved.

Scripture quotations marked NASB are taken from the New American Standard Bible®, Copyright © 1960, 1962, 1963, 1968, 1971, 1972, 1973, 1975, 1977, 1995 by The Lockman Foundation. Used by permission. (www.Lockman.org)

Scripture quotations marked CEV are from the Contemporary English Version Copyright © 1991, 1992, 1995 by American Bible Society. Used by Permission.

FaithWords
Hachette Book Group
237 Park Avenue
New York, NY 10017

www.faithwords.com

Printed in the United States of America

RRD-C

First Large Print Edition: May 2014
10 9 8 7 6 5 4 3 2 1

FaithWords is a division of Hachette Book Group, Inc.
The FaithWords name and logo are trademarks of Hachette Book Group, Inc.

The Hachette Speakers Bureau provides a wide range of authors for speaking events. To find out more, go to www.hachettespeakersbureau.com or call (866) 376-6591.

The publisher is not responsible for websites (or their content) that are not owned by the publisher.

Library of Congress Cataloging-in-Publication Data

Dollar, Creflo A.
  Real manhood : being the man God made you to be / Dr. Creflo Dollar.—First Edition.
    pages cm
  ISBN 978-1-4555-7798-9 (hardcover)—ISBN 978-1-4555-8206-8 (large print hardcover)—ISBN 978-1-4789-5314-2 (audiobook)—ISBN 978-1-4789-5315-9 (audio download)—ISBN 978-1-4555-7800-9 (ebook) 1. Men (Christian theology) 2. Christian men—Religious life. 3. Christian men—Conduct of life. I. Title.
  BT703.5.D65 2014
  248.8'42—dc23

2013043012

CONTENTS

Stand firm in your faith... **Act like men** and
be courageous; grow in strength!

—1 CORINTHIANS 16:13 (AMP)

INTRODUCTION

I often think about men and the issues we have. After many years spent counseling men, studying the Word of God, and cultivating my own development into real manhood, I am finally writing a book for men and about men. I am going to dig deep and take an unflinching look at the state of manhood. I believe there has been a calculated assault on manhood in modern society, which is why we are experiencing a generation of fatherless young men who are struggling to find their significance. Sexual promiscuity, violence, drug abuse, insecurity, depression, suicidal ideation, and lack of preparedness for the future are all symptoms of a deeper issue.

I want to point out that I didn't write this book to say there are no more good men. That's a lie. There are many good men. Neither did I write this book to beat up on men and tear them down any more than they already have been. Instead, I wrote this book by the inspiration of the Holy Spirit to affect the man who knows he has not yet become what he was meant to be. We can be better than we are. Yet the world and the lies of the enemy have convinced many men that they are stuck. It's all simply untrue. It reminds me of an old quote I heard, "You can't keep a man down who has in him the yeast to rise."

God never creates a man for a life of disappointment and struggle.

God never creates a man for a life of disappointment and struggle. He created us to dominate and to be a reflection of Himself in the earth. And since God never loses, we are not supposed to lose either.

We're going to go on this journey together. We're going to look at the intent God had in mind when he decided to create a man. We must do this. The Bible says "If the foundations are removed, what can the righteous do?" So we are going to return to the source and gain God's vision for our lives as men.

However, I want to warn you. In order for us to go higher together, we are going to have to shine the light on every issue, sin, hurt, pain, fear, excuse, religious tradition, failure, and negative thought. Then we must have the courage to believe we have the ability to go beyond the limitations of our past. God has given us His grace, in order to be the men He's called us to be. This grace goes beyond just forgiveness of our sins. This grace is the very power of

God that enables us to be strong men when we are weak in our own ability. And believe me, we need God in order to be real men. Therefore, I encourage you to let that truth ring loud on the inside of you right now. Also, before you turn the page and go further in this book, I want you to understand that only a man who relies on God is a real man. A man becomes a man when he realizes he, in and of himself, is weak and needs God to do what only He can do.

Only a man who relies on God is a real man.

So I'm excited about your discovering what God has already completed and made available for your life. You no longer have to be discouraged, because everything you need has already been provided. You simply have to take a step of faith to receive the vision God has for your life. I promise you won't regret it.

1

THE ORIGIN OF A MAN

And God said, Let us make man in our image, after our likeness: and let them have dominion over the fish of the sea, and over the fowl of the air, and over the cattle, and over all the earth, and over every creeping thing that creepeth upon the earth.

—GENESIS 1:26

The steps of a good man are ordered by the LORD: and he delighteth in his way.

—PSALM 37:23

When you look at the origin of a thing, you are uncovering the original purpose and intent of its creator. This is important because when you don't understand the purpose of anything abuse is inevitable. So, in order to uncover the purpose of a man you must return to the source.

When I originally considered writing this book, I had planned to dive right into the many issues men deal with. However, the Lord gave me insight on how grave a mistake that would be, and, instead, instructed me to start at the beginning.

The book of Genesis is one of my favorite books in the Bible. It is the book of beginnings. Everything that has ever been created has its origin there. *Webster's Dictionary* defines the word *origin* as *something from which anything arises or is derived; source.* Another definition I like is *to rise from a particular source, or first stage of existence.* With this understanding, the first words in the book of Genesis are *In the beginning God...* These could be the most powerful words in the Bible.

*Everything we can see and cannot see was
formed and created by God.*

Everything began with God. He is the foundation of it all. He created the heavens and the earth. Everything we can see and cannot see was formed and created by God. Verse 3 in Genesis gives us insight into how God made everything he created. *And God said.* Three very simple words, but in them we see all of the creative ability of God manifested. God's ability to create is released in what He said. The next several verses show Him speaking into existence everything—the earth, animals, vegetation, oceans, skies, seasons, and so on.

Each thing God spoke into existence got His stamp of approval. He said it, He saw it, then declared it was good. But God chose not to stop there. As glorious as everything was that He had created in the physical realm, there was one last work of creation that needed to be fulfilled. It would no doubt be God's greatest flourish of creativity, power, and skill. He decided to make a man.

Who Is Man?

As He did with everything else He created, God spoke what His desire and design was for man. "And God said, Let us make man in our image, after our likeness: and let them have dominion..." (Genesis 1:26).

This scripture highlights two very specific things when it comes to revealing the purpose for every man in life. First, God created us in His image and to be like Him, as an exact reflection and representation of Himself. Second, God created men to have dominion. The word *dominion* means power, the right to govern and rule over a particular area; to have absolute mastery. This is not something to be taken lightly. God made men like Him and gave us the same absolute mastery *over all the earth*. This means, in God's original intent for man, nothing was created that was not submitted under the authority God invested in man.

When God created man to be just like Him,
man had to have power and dominion
the same way God does.

In other words, when God created man to be just like Him, man had to have power and dominion the same way God does. Therefore, He extended His power and authority to both the man and woman. As such, no one other than God was above man in terms of rank and order. God was number one and just below Him was man.

Also, it is interesting to note here that when God spoke these words over man He had not yet created man's physical body from the dust of the ground, which means man was still in the spirit realm with God. Before man was manifested in the physical realm, God already had a clear image of him and identity for him, and even spoke His vision over man before he was *born* into the earth realm.

In fact, all of creation is so overshadowed by the magnificence of man that in Psalm 8:4 we see the declaration of pure astonishment: "What is man that thou art mindful of him? And the son of man, that thou visitest him?" In modern-day vernacular this verse says, "Wow, what is this? What's a man? He's so special and unique that God thinks about him all the time. And not only that, you visit him, too!" Hebrews 2:5–8 even confirms that the angels in heaven were amazed at man; one of them couldn't resist asking God the same question that was asked in Psalm 8.

Remember, God created man to have dominion.

It doesn't stop there. Remember, God created man to have dominion. I looked very carefully at the next verse of scripture in Psalm 8, which reads:

For thou has made him a little lower than the angels.

(PSALM 8:5)

This verse gives insight into the present-day challenges you may be having as a man. You may be thinking, "What does that have to do with what I'm facing right now?" The answer is *everything*.

In order to receive insight, we must understand that the Bible was originally written in Hebrew and translated into other languages. However, translators mistranslated a word in Psalm 8:5, and changing one word changes the entire meaning of the scripture, which can cloud God's original intent. The word *angel* in verse 5, when translated back to the original Hebrew, is the word *Elohim* or *God*. Therefore, in the original Hebrew verse 5 reads: "For God has created man a little lower than God or Himself." It is imperative that you gain a concept of this truth, or you will never reach your full potential as a man.

Over the years, the religious mind-set has fought this truth and dismissed it as heresy. Satan, over the centuries, has done everything he can to attack anyone who has tried to shed light on this truth. But, as Christians, we make the Bible our final authority, and all argument stops there. Psalm 8:5, in the original Hebrew, reveals God's intention for a man. Further, the creation of man could be considered God's tour de force of creative genius that can never be rivaled or equaled. He made a man just like Himself, with His dominion and authority in the earth realm, and the man was second in command only to God Himself!

Like man, angels are also created beings. However, angels do not have ranking authority over men. The order is God—man—angels. If you can receive this, you can understand why the devil does not want you to realize this. Satan is also an angelic being, which means he and all other angelic beings are beneath man in terms of rank. Angels have a type of glory, but man surpassed the angels. Man was crowned with God's own glory and set in charge over all the works of His hands (Psalm 8:5–6).

Man was crowned with God's own glory and set in charge over all the works of His hands.

I know many of you have probably not heard this taught in the traditional church. For this very reason, we don't see the church at the level of glory God prophesied. God called the church glorious. However, our true identity has been hidden from us. Now, if you look at this in terms of true manhood, you will begin to discover why men are not operating in their rightful place. Instead of ruling and reigning, they are being ruled by life and its circumstances. But this was never what God intended for you as men. The Bible says He put all things under our feet (Psalm 8:6), which means we are supposed to be walking above our challenges.

So the next question you may have is, "If God created me in His image and gave me authority, why don't I have it?" Continuing further in the book of Genesis will give you the answer.

As the history of man begins to unfold in the book of Genesis, we see that God formed Adam first from the dust of the ground. "And the Lord God formed man of the dust of the ground, and breathed into his nostrils the breath of life; and man became a living soul" (Genesis 2:7).

If you've been to church, you've heard this scripture before. But I believe few people live in the power of this scripture in their everyday lives. It's almost become a religious cliché that many have no working revelation of in their lives. Christians and sinners alike have missed the heart of God on how truly magnificent God originally made man. The present state of warped manhood is a result of this missed truth.

Christians and sinners alike have missed the heart of God on how truly magnificent God originally made man.

Recently, I ran across quotes by two very famous authors from American literature that echo the same lie concerning our identity. One quote says:

Man was made at the end of the week's work when God was tired.

And the other one says:

I think that God, in creating man, somewhat overestimated his ability.

I will admit that I found them humorous until the Spirit of God spoke very clearly and sternly to my heart. He said:

"This same attitude and lie has been passed down throughout the ages and is not a laughing matter. There are unsaved men who have no idea of their true purpose and identity. They're dead and don't even know it. And even My own people have such a warped and low view of themselves that they struggle to believe Me for what I've already done for them. But I'm raising up an army of men who know their worth and identity in Me. By their very nature, they will bring deliverance and freedom to mankind."

Looking more closely at Genesis 2:7, we can see a key phrase. "God *breathed* into his nostrils the breath of life, and man became a living soul." I did a detailed study of this one portion of scripture, and what I learned was truly fascinating. When God breathed the breath of life into the nostrils of Adam, He placed everything in him that makes God who He is. Literally, God took His own essence and placed it inside the man. His eternal nature and life was released from Himself into Adam. Man was alive and became a living soul. The Hebrew Bible says *man became another speaking spirit.*

When God breathed the breath of life into the nostrils of Adam, He placed everything in him that makes God who He is.

Ultimately, Genesis 2:7 reveals not only that man was made in God's image, giving him the right to rule, but that he was also fully possessed with God's nature. And, to top it off, man had the same creative ability as God, to speak and then see what he said.

The Plot Thickens

After the creation of Adam, things continued to unfold. God placed the man in the beautiful and lush Garden of Eden, which means *abundant and voluptuous living.* The garden was *perfect.* God didn't place Adam in a place of barrenness. He put him in a place of provision and abundance. I believe it is safe to say that this is what God desired the man to have from the very beginning, and His desire has not changed.

It is in the Garden of Eden that God revealed His first intention for the man, which was to dress and keep the garden. Other translations use the words *care for, guard,* and *keep order.* However, in the mind of God, a man who bears His image and has His authority and creative ability should bring order and uphold things in the way God originally intended. Literally, Adam was God's enforcer on the earth. This was his work.

After man was placed in the garden and given the responsibility to care for it, God gave him instructions on how to live. He told Adam that he had freedom, with established boundaries. "Of every tree of the garden thou mayest freely eat. But of the tree of knowledge of good and evil, thou shalt not eat…thou shalt surely die" (Genesis 2:16–17). This scripture reveals the other intent God had in mind for man.

It is God's will for man to receive his blueprint and instructions for life from his Creator.

It is God's will for man to receive his blueprint and instructions for life from his Creator. This is the only way he can truly learn how to govern life. God wanted Adam to learn from the very beginning that remaining within the established boundaries meant freedom and delight in Eden. However, stepping outside of those boundaries meant death (spiritual separation from God). Men, please know that, in this present day and time, the inevitability of that truth has not changed. Your freedom and delight in life are within the boundaries and instructions God has given for your life. Therefore, I encourage you to look at your life, and if it is nothing like Eden, begin to make the necessary adjustments.

After giving Adam his work assignment and instructions for life, God takes Adam through what I like to call "god-training." God literally created all the animals from the same ground from which he formed the man, but He didn't name them. Of course He could have named the animals Himself, but God wanted the man to exercise his God-given authority in the earth realm. Just as God spoke over Adam and released the breath of life into him, it was Adam's turn to do the same with the animals. Genesis 2:19 states: "And out of the ground the LORD God formed every beast of the field, and every fowl of the air; and brought them unto Adam to see what he would call them: and *whatsoever Adam called every living creature, that was the name thereof.*" Adam literally called into life every species of animal. Can you imagine the kind of wisdom Adam had to possess in order to do that?

In a nutshell, this is the progression of God's intent for the man: He gave the man identity, dominion, and authority (the right to rule), established boundaries and clear instructions on how to live and work, gave him the assignment to enforce His will on earth, and made him aware of the fact that he was just like God—filled with wisdom and creative ability.

*The creation story in Genesis makes it
absolutely clear that God had a purpose
and a plan for man.*

The creation story in Genesis makes it absolutely clear that God had a purpose and a plan for man. However, it is interesting to note that it wasn't until the man had been established in his dominion and authority that God mentioned the woman. Once Adam was operating in his rightful place, the Bible states: "And the LORD God said, It is not good that the man should be alone; I will make him a help meet for him" (Genesis 2:18).

God does something different when He creates the woman. She is not created from the dust of the ground, like Adam. The Bible says that God caused a sleep to come over the man. He took a piece of the man—one of his ribs—and made the woman. Then God simply presents her to the man. Adam, once again, does the same thing he did with the animals that God presented to him. He pronounces words over the woman and even proclaims, with the authority God gave him, the purpose of a man and woman coming together.

"And Adam said, This is now bone of my bones, and flesh of my flesh: she shall be called woman, because she was taken out of man. Therefore, shall a man leave his father and his mother, and shall cleave unto his wife: and they shall be one flesh" (Genesis 2:23–24).

Adam was God's mouthpiece when he proclaimed the Word of God over the very first marriage.

Operating in his God-given authority, Adam was God's mouthpiece when he proclaimed the Word of God over the very first marriage. Further, this marriage was nothing short of perfection. The man and woman were together, naked, and unashamed in God's presence—the pinnacle of all God's creation.

What we can gain from the creation story up to this point is far-reaching, to say the least. However, one particular point I want you to see, as it relates to the man and woman, is *the man was in his right position and had the vision to see and receive the woman God presented.* I will go into further detail about this later in the book, when I talk about a man and his woman.

The Tragedy of Man's Fall

In Genesis 3:1, the devil—man's enemy—enters the garden disguised as a serpent. He was once known as Lucifer—the anointed cherub—who was responsible for praise in heaven. This fallen angel sees the magnificence and glory of the man God created, and *he hates it*. Why? He knows that man is what he is not—*the very image of God*. So, he moves with subtlety and deceit to attack this god-man and woman. It's the same attack he brings against every man in this present time. He launches his attacks in your mind, will, and emotions to cause you to disconnect from the instructions God gave you.

The enemy knew that Adam was covered with the glory of God, which was the very presence of God Himself.

The enemy knew that Adam was covered with the glory of God, which was the very presence of God Himself. So he figured out how to get Adam to forfeit the authority God had given him. However, the devil had no right or authority to take it because God had put all things under man's feet, which included the devil and all demons. So the devil plants subtle seeds of doubt to cause Adam and Eve to believe they weren't what God made them to be.

Genesis 3:1–7 reads:

And he said unto the woman, Yea, hath God said, Ye shall not eat of every tree of the garden?

And the woman said unto the serpent, We may eat of the fruit of the trees of the garden:

But of the fruit of the tree which is in the midst of the garden, God hath said, Ye shall not eat of it, neither shall ye touch it, lest ye die.

And the serpent said unto the woman, Ye shall not surely die:

For God doth know that in the day ye eat thereof, then your eyes shall be opened, and ye shall be as gods, knowing good and evil.

And when the woman saw that the tree was good for food, and that it was pleasant to the eyes, and a tree to be desired to make one wise, she took of the fruit thereof, and did eat, and gave also unto her husband with her; and he did eat.

And the eyes of them both were opened, and they knew that they were naked; and they sewed fig leaves together, and made themselves aprons.

Please take particular notice of verses 4 and 5. Satan told the man and woman, "You're not going to die." We know this was a lie, because earlier in Genesis we read where God gave clear instructions to the man. Not only did he lie to them, he made them doubt God's goodness by making them think God was holding out on them. Have you noticed in your own life that every temptation—no matter how it comes or where it leads—is always laced with the false promise that you will gain either something that God doesn't want you to have or something He is withholding from you? That's the trick of the enemy at work.

Once the man and woman were opened to the enemy's suggestion, their emotions began to take over.

Once the man and woman were opened to the enemy's suggestion, their emotions began to take over. The Bible says that Eve saw the tree as pleasant, good, and to be desired. So she ate and then gave it to the man to eat. Please don't disregard the fact that Adam was standing right there when Eve was tempted. However, he was passive and did not stand in his place of authority against the enemy's attack. I believe Adam's passive behavior birthed many of man's challenges of today. Emotions and fleshly desires rule, rather than obedience to the Word of God, and the list goes on. However, I will delve further into this as we continue our journey.

The Consequences of Taking the Bait

Adam and Eve ate the fruit, and it was in direct rebellion against what God had instructed. As a result, their eyes were opened and they saw the world in a different light—having the knowledge of good and evil. The man and his woman realized they were naked and uncovered, and they felt the need to cover themselves. Why? They were no longer unashamed. Sin will always bring shame. However, most important, what really happened was that they lost the glory of God. They were no longer covered with His tangible presence. Before the fall, Adam and Eve didn't have artificial clothing. They were literally covered with God, but once they sinned they realized they were no longer clothed. The scriptures go on to say that God came looking for the man. "And the Lord God called unto Adam, and said unto him, Where art thou?" (Genesis 3:9). Notice God spoke directly to the man first. Before we go any further, I want to point out that God didn't ask that question because He needed an answer. Neither was He asking where Adam was in terms of locality. He already knew where Adam was. He asked the question so that Adam could fully realize where he was and how far he had fallen. God knew Adam had stepped out of his position and rightful place of authority. And, to make matters worse, the authority he had once possessed had been turned over to the devil—man's enemy.

The man's response to God's question is probably the saddest recorded passage in the entire Bible. Genesis 3:10 states: "And he said, I heard thy voice in the garden, and I was afraid, because I was naked; and I hid myself." Think about it. This was the man who was second in command to God, covered in the tangible presence of God, and eternal, like God. Adam was the pinnacle of God's creation. However, because of sin, he found himself hiding behind a bush, covered in fear and shame.

---

*Adam was the pinnacle of God's creation.
However, because of sin, he found
himself hiding behind a bush, covered
in fear and shame.*

Up until that point of their existence, all Adam and Eve had ever experienced was the presence of God. However, as a result of disobedience to God, they had become fallen creatures, stained by sin. Nevertheless, because of God's love for them, He still showed up to talk to them as usual. Genesis 3:11–12 states: "And he said, Who told thee that thou wast naked? Hast thou eaten of the tree, whereof I commanded thee that thou shouldest not eat? And the man said, The woman whom thou gavest to be with me, she gave me of the tree, and I did eat."

Again, God knew the answer before He asked the question. He simply wanted Adam to understand the reason why he was now in a state he had never been in before. Sin had taken Adam outside of the realm of power, love, and the presence of God into a state of fear and death.

What was the man's response? He blamed his woman (Genesis 3:12). He failed to take responsibility for their actions. I honestly believe that if Adam had taken responsibility and asked for God's forgiveness, it would have all ended right there. Since he didn't do so, a curse was released into the earth and on man. A curse is simply an empowerment to fail. Sadly, all that was blissful and perfect had been marred by sin and the curse.

Now you may be thinking, *I thought God said they were going to die, yet they were still alive.* We have to understand what death is from God's perspective and what really died that day. Obviously, the death that took place couldn't have been physical, or they would have both dropped dead right then. So what died?

---

*God, who is a Spirit, created man in his
image to live eternally.*

God, who is a Spirit, created man in his image
to live eternally. Please understand, man is a tri-part
being—he is a spirit, who has a soul (mind, will, and
emotions), and lives in a physical body. Therefore,
the death God was speaking of was not a physical
death, but a spiritual death, which is separation from
God. Adam's spirit died that day. And, as a result,
his physical body was no longer immortal.

Out of love for them, God drove the man and
woman out of the Garden of Eden and His presence. He drove them out of the garden so that they
wouldn't eat from the tree of life again. This may
seem like God was just being cruel, but that wasn't
the case. Had they eaten from the tree of life again,
they would have been stuck in that sinful state
for eternity. So removing the man and woman from
the garden was actually an act of love and mercy.
Further, they could no longer be in His presence,
because the presence of God is destructive to sin.

Because of man's fall in the garden, the entire
human race is changed forever. Every man that is
born is connected to the sin that Adam committed
in the garden. Every man, woman, and child born

on this planet is shaped in iniquity and conceived in sin (Psalm 51:5). Every man starts his journey on this planet from this place. There are no exceptions to this. If you are born into this world, you are automatically connected to Adam's sin.

God Has Another Plan for Man

God, in His infinite wisdom, knew everything that was going to happen with His creation. He had a plan before the foundation of the world and had no intention of leaving the crown jewel of all creation in a state of sin and death.

God is love, and He created man for relationship with Him.

God is love, and He created man for relationship with Him. However, sin and God cannot exist in the same place. God had to devise a plan that would redeem man back to Himself. That plan is Jesus and the Gospel. The good news is simply that God sent Jesus to pay the price and take on all of man's sin and iniquity. Jesus' sacrifice meant that God put the penalty of our sin on Jesus and extended His righteousness to all men. When Jesus died on the cross, the penalty for sin was satisfied. When He rose He defeated sin, death, and the devil forever. Jesus was perfectly sinless, and now God declares that any man who believes in Him can be reborn or born-again, from the spiritual death that came from Adam's sin to life again in Jesus.

This has been provided for all men. Any man who simply believes in Jesus is now spiritually alive again, and the Spirit of God moves into His spirit. He gains Jesus' righteousness and is back in right standing with God. In Christ, a man literally is placed in the same exalted status Adam was in before the fall.

Therefore, before I go any further, there is a decision you must make, because your journey to real manhood cannot begin until you are in right standing with God through a personal relationship with Jesus. You will spend your life living only a mere glimpse of what you could have been. Further, the devil will do everything he can to keep you blind to this truth. He may allow you to be exalted and have a form of success in this world, but his ultimate goal is to make sure your journey is filled with torment and that you miss the destination God has planned for your life.

If you are a man who has already accepted Jesus

as your Lord, but you are still living far below the privileges God desires for you, it's not too late to make a change. Simply that you are reading this book is an indication that something in you wants to change. You are definitely on the right path. Be encouraged and know that everything you've ever desired for your life has already been completed in Jesus. So you don't have to beg God for what He has already provided for you in Christ. He simply wants you to willingly go on a faith journey and believe it's already yours.

Be encouraged and know that everything you've ever desired for your life has already been completed in Jesus.

As our journey continues, I will show you the implications and meanings for your life based on the Word of God. Are you ready? If so, here we go.

2

FAILING TO MEASURE UP

But if any provide not for his own, and specially for those of his own house, he hath denied the faith, and is worse than an infidel.

—1 TIMOTHY 5:8

He hath shewed thee, O man, what is good; and what doth the LORD require of thee, but to do justly, and to love mercy, and to walk humbly with thy God?

—MICAH 6:8

There are some men who are even driven or paralyzed by a persistent thought that they do not measure up. Then, there are other men who feel superior yet they don't realize they are still not what they were meant to be. The only way to avoid both extremes is to realize God is all you need.

I believe it's so important for men to understand the progression of things and how things happen because *nothing just happens.* Everything happens for a reason. For instance, the current condition of your life is a result of your past decisions and actions. But that's only on the surface. If you really want to know the foundation of the decisions and actions that are responsible for your current place in life, you must understand the internal motivating factors. The external circumstance is only the tip of the iceberg. The real question is what has been hibernating and brooding beneath the surface.

In all my years of pastoring and counseling, I have learned that men don't like to deal with the internal things.

Know thyself is an ancient Greek aphorism. The Bible talks about truth in the inner part of man (Psalm 51:6). In all my years of pastoring and counseling, I have learned that men don't like to deal with the internal things. Maybe it is because we deem it a feminine characteristic, or we are simply afraid to do so. However, I've noticed that most men are more comfortable covering up than taking a look inside.

As I mentioned in the previous chapter, every issue a man deals with in life can be traced back to the book of Genesis. Further, there is one root issue that is common to *every* man—an inferiority complex. You don't hear too many men talk about it in today's society, but we can see the manifestation of it scattered across the landscape of their lives. If we are going to be the men God called us to be, we must understand and get rid of feelings of inferiority.

What is an inferiority complex? It is a persistent sense of feeling as though you fail to measure up. It's a persistent sense of inadequacy and a tendency toward self-deprecation. It can also be defined as feeling lower in rank, status, or accomplishments than one's counterparts. Based on these definitions, you can see why many men don't talk about or deal with this issue. Unfortunately, in most cases, a feeling of inferiority is one of those things a man doesn't necessarily know he is dealing with. Or, if he is aware that he struggles in this area, it's not something he is likely to admit. No man wants to admit that he feels uncertain and unsure about himself. I interact with many young men, and I can tell by the way they carry themselves that they lack a sense of validation. As a result, they are insecure and have a strong drive or need for individual accomplishments.

---

*No man wants to admit that he feels
uncertain and unsure about himself.*

I experienced this in my own life. I remember when I was a young pastor just starting my ministry. I thought I had to prove myself and impress people. There were other preachers who had been in ministry a lot longer than I had; I mean they could *preach.* I felt I had to do everything they were doing instead of just being myself. Because of a constant dread of falling short, I felt I needed to feel accomplished in this area. It was pure bondage. I am grateful I don't deal with those crippling feelings of inferiority anymore. God freed me.

Now, on another level, I don't want you to think that having a high degree of accomplishment guarantees you freedom from feelings of inferiority. In fact, I've met many successful men, and as I began to spend time with them, I realized they were exhibiting symptoms of an inferiority complex. Sometimes, men who are very accomplished have a lot more "trimmings" that cover up their feelings of falling short. They are able to use their accomplishments and possessions to camouflage feelings of inferiority that they try to keep hidden within themselves.

The inferiority complex was one of the first curses brought upon man as a result of the fall. As such, this is a giant that every man must face. Remember what Adam did immediately after he sinned? He ran and hid because he was uncovered and afraid. In other words, he felt as if he was falling short.

A man who constantly deals with feelings of inferiority, or is constantly hiding, is a man who never seems to break out of his shell. As a result, all the gifts and abilities he has lie dormant within him because he is so consumed by his own insecurities. He feels unable to go beyond his own self-imposed barriers. He also tends to overcompensate and hide behind expensive clothes and a large bank account. However, at night when he's alone, he is still tormented by an unspoken yet still tangible anxiety about himself that no amount of external trimmings can erase.

> *The truth is, a man cannot reach his full stature without understanding* the why *behind* the what.

The truth is, a man cannot reach his full stature without understanding *the why* behind *the what*. This is one of the key deceptions the devil loves to play on men. He would rather we waste years trying to break an external bad habit like alcoholism, overeating, or sexual sin without ever trying to find out the root cause of it in the first place. This is the key reason why many men never truly experience the level of freedom God created us to have. They are too busy fighting against the outer enemy, not realizing the issue was birthed from another source.

There are many symptoms of inferiority, and how you answer the following questions can help you determine if you are dealing with it.

Do you have a hard time admitting your weaknesses, while easily pointing out the weaknesses of others?

Do you bully or exert yourself over other people with disdain?

Do you feel personally attacked when someone disagrees with you?

Do you feel belittled as a person when someone corrects or confronts you? Do you blame others for your problems?

Do you derive your worth from your appearance, wealth, performance, or accomplishments?

Are you easily hurt? Are you critical or defensive?

Do you go over and above to get others to like and accept you? Or worse yet, do you pretend you don't need anyone at all?

Do you boast about yourself and your accomplishments?

The media have conditioned young men to idolize these men who are on the top of the mountain.

I particularly want to focus on the last question. In today's society, we see a lot of this. There are men who have a high level of outward success, and are usually at the top of their fields. The media have conditioned young men to idolize these men who are on the top of the mountain. This is understandable, because they appear to have it all. A young man who is struggling to find his way in the world will find this very attractive. So, like a magnet, he is drawn to the images of what appear to be examples of a real man. Yet from God's perspective—that of the One who can see everything—the men who are idolized as the "kings of this world" are sorely lacking in many important areas and are not true models for young men to follow.

Our enemy the devil knows this as well. His method of operation is very simple. He doesn't mind our being elevated in the eyes of the world. He'll allow us to prosper outwardly and to build a fortress that seems impenetrable from man's perspective. Yet God knows it's all on a shaky foundation. Jesus gave a very strong perspective on this in Revelation 3:17–18 (NLT).

> *You say, "I am rich. I have everything I want. I don't need a thing!" And you don't realize that you are wretched and miserable and poor and blind and naked. So I advise you to buy gold from me—gold that has been purified by fire. Then you will be rich. Also buy white garments from me so you will not be shamed by your nakedness, and ointment for your eyes so you will be able to see.*

Here we see what defines this man's security. It is actually false security, because it is not built on God's way of doing things. From God's perspective, no matter how high we climb in the world's eye, without Him we will end up uncovered, naked, and hiding behind a tree in shame like Adam, when he was disconnected from God.

So what's the answer? Even with the definitions I've given you for inferiority, we still have to get a biblical perspective on what is truly at the root of inferiority. There's a very familiar verse of scripture I want to look at, Romans 3:23: "For all have sinned, and come short of the glory of God." The Apostle Paul was talking about the righteousness of God, which is available to all men by faith in Jesus. Every man is born into sin but through Christ we can be righteous.

Every man is born into sin but through Christ we can be righteous.

In regards to the inferiority issue, I want you to focus in on the last few words of Romans 3:23: "Come short of the glory of God." What does it mean to come short of the glory of God, in a practical sense? It means to fail to become all God intended us to be, or to be less than what God has created us to be. That is the essence of all inferiority. The New Living Translation of this same verse gives even greater insight: "Everyone has sinned, and we all fall short of God's glorious standard." What causes us to fall short of all we were meant to be and God's standard? One word—sin.

Sin is a word we avoid using in today's secular culture. We now call it our "problem" or "issue." We dare not say the word *sin* because the word, in and of itself, reminds us that we are out of sync with God. On the other end of the spectrum, the church and Christians are so sin-conscious that inferiority seems to always have a foothold in the lives of many.

Here is what I want you to see. The scripture says everyone has sinned and is now inferior to God's plan. Does this mean the bad act you did yesterday caused you to be inferior? To a certain degree, but that's not what this scripture is talking about. This scripture is talking about the original sin in the Garden of Eden. Every man has sinned *in Adam*. So when you were born—the very first day you entered the world—you were immediately born into sin and inferiority. There is no getting around this fact.

So imagine going through life in a state of sin and living below God's standard if you are dealing with inferiority. Even if you are an extremely successful man outwardly, you are still living far below God's standard as a man if you are constantly struggling with feelings of inadequacy. However, if you get hold of the answer I'm about to share, you can come out of inferiority.

Even if you are an extremely successful man outwardly, you are still living far below God's standard as a man if you are constantly struggling with feelings of inadequacy.

John 1:29 is one verse of scripture that reveals the answer to the problem.

"The next day John seeth Jesus coming unto him, and saith, Behold the Lamb of God, which taketh away the sin of the world." Jesus has dealt with the root issue of inferiority—sin! Now that He has paid the price for sin, in Him we can be free. I want you to notice something. When do Christian men feel the most inferior? It is when we've done something we know violates God's Word. The enemy counts on us remaining in emotional heaviness and condemnation, which increases our feelings of falling short. But because of Jesus, we have the right, as Believers, to boldly declare our righteousness, and that all of our sins—past, present, and future—have already been forgiven through Christ. So there is nothing our adversary can hold over our heads. All we have to do is repent, turn, and go in the right direction.

Jesus has done everything that was needed to accomplish our freedom. However, we need to know what to do in order to be in line with what's already been finished. Here are a few practical things you can do to conquer inferiority.

Find and follow God's plan for your life. Finding and obeying the will of God for your life is critical if you are going to be free from inferiority. The desire and will of God is the place where you'll shine, and your creativity and genius will be revealed to the world. I come into contact with many men who struggle to know the specific will of God for their lives. I always like to point them to the simplest truth. God's Word is His will. I tell them to start there. When you live in line with the Word and change your thinking to agree with what His Word says, you open up an avenue through which God can become more specific when giving you instructions for the tailor-made calling He has placed on your life.

The desire and will of God is the place where you'll shine, and your creativity and genius will be revealed to the world.

Don't be discouraged. God wouldn't begin to work in you if He wasn't going to bring His plan to full completion. He can take you from where you are right now and bring you to the fullness of where He has always envisioned you to be.

Being confident of this very thing, that he which hath begun a good work in you will perform it until the day of Jesus Christ.

(PHILIPPIANS 1:6)

Develop your image by the measure of God's Word. The best way for a man to build himself up is by viewing himself and his life by God's measurement—His Word. Something happens when you take on God's thoughts concerning you. This will require you to spend time in the Word and pray, which are vital if your inner image of yourself is going to change. Measuring your life by the Word takes the focus off yourself and places it on others. I've never met a self-centered man who wasn't inferior in some way. However, as you spend more time in prayer and the Word, you'll find yourself extending more and more to help other people. This was always God's intent for a man—to move beyond himself to serve others. There's a saying that goes, "A man who can't go beyond himself is his own worst enemy." Make sure your perspective is focused on what God says about you, and from that foundation, begin to extend yourself to others.

Put all of your abilities and gifts at God's disposal. A man who totally opens himself to God on a daily basis will find that more is available to him in return. God brightens the dullness in your life when the abilities He's given you are being used for Him. Every man has gifts. There are things you do that are unique to you. Sure, there may be another person who does the same thing you do, but God made only *one you*. God wants the world to experience the gifts He has given you. Even if there are millions of other people who seem to have the same gift as you, from God's perspective, the world is lacking if it has not experienced what *you* have to offer. Make sharing your gift with those around you a priority every day.

God wants the world to experience the gifts
He has given you.

Get rid of all delusions of grandeur and comparisons with others. Let me paint a picture for you. There's a man who has a vision of being a great, well-known, and world-class authority in business. He knows he received the vision from God. So he sets all his sights on the end of the vision. However, he spends so much time focusing on the grandeur of the big vision that he doesn't take the small, practical, day-to-day steps of obedience to get there. As time goes by, he seems to be further and further from what God showed him. He becomes discouraged. As a result, he feels shorter in stature as a man than he ever has, as he looks at other men who are prospering in the very thing he was supposed to do. This slowly begins to take its toll on his soul. He increasingly becomes more frustrated, while still neglecting the "little things" that could bring him closer to achieving his goal. While he is looking for the big event, he has failed to realize the big event is in the small daily acts of obedience.

I can't tell you how many men I've counseled who have lived this scenario, including me. I experienced this in my own ministry. God told me at the very beginning that my ministry would be worldwide. However, it was only when I stopped focusing on the big vision, and realized I needed to enjoy the journey by paying attention to the "little things" that would eventually get me there, that I became an all-around better man. I became a man who was focused and directed rather than driven.

Preparation plus opportunity always leads to success.

If you can identify, you can make the adjustments today by taking your eyes off everyone else around you, and where they appear to be, versus where you are. Simply focus on what you can do today. Jesus made it very clear that greatness comes from small beginnings. Why? Through small beginnings, God builds character in a man, which will sustain him when he reaches the mountaintop. God isn't in the business of bringing men to the top and then letting them fall. That's the devil's method of operation. God wants you to be able to remain in the place He has prepared for you. Preparation plus opportunity always leads to success. Ask yourself what you can do today to prepare. If you are faithful and obedient where you are, God can trust you when you walk in His overflowing abundance. Before we move on, I want to once again express the importance of dealing with the inferiority issue. God didn't create you to fail or fall short. He created you for success. However, failure to realize that you've been created in the image and likeness of God and to find your identity in Christ leads to a life of falling short of all you were meant to be, which ultimately leads to something I'd like to call fabrication. Let's go a little further and discover how this affects a man's life.

3

THE FABRICATED MAN

Lo, this only have I found, that God hath
made man upright; but they have sought
out many inventions.

—ECCLESIASTES 7:29

We are all one man's sons; we are true men...

—GENESIS 42:11

But he that is greatest among you
shall be your servant.

—MATTHEW 23:11

When the image and mask a man hides behind is shattered to pieces, he is finally ready to truly live. Anything short of this is a crutch and a manufactured lie.

I want you to understand the world in which we live, and the deceptive traps the enemy has set for you. The devil wants you to downgrade or overestimate yourself, be overwhelmed with insecurity, and question your manhood. His ultimate goal is for you to think you are a real man and spend your entire life looking like a success in the eyes of others, only to be a failure as a man from God's perspective. It doesn't matter to him which category you fall into, as long as you never reach God's will for your life. He actually doesn't care if you're born again and going to heaven. What he doesn't want is to see you gain enough light to ultimately affect someone else's life.

Why do you think it's been such a struggle for you? Because it really isn't about you. There is someone you were called to reach, affect, and help to get to his or her destination in life. However, many men are confused when it comes to their own lives. The darkness and fog they seem unable to see through is meant to keep them contained.

We need light to break the walls of containment around our lives. No man ever rises without light. Light is simply understanding and wisdom. When a man gains the light of God's Word, he will finally see things the way God sees them.

When a man gains the light of God's Word, he will finally see things the way God sees them.

"My heart panteth, my strength faileth me: as for the light of mine eyes, it also is gone from me" (Psalm 38:10). A man who has no light or wisdom becomes weary, and his strength fails him. Life wears a man down when he is constantly facing challenges, and he sees no way out. I've discovered there is a type of man that life wears down very quickly—the *fabricated* man.

What does it mean when something is fabricated? Look at the root word *fabric*. One definition of the word *fabric* is *the method of construction*. This gives us some interesting insight. When a man is fabricated, he has constructed the image of himself that he wants to portray to the outside world, except it's not his true self. It's a carefully constructed, invented, and forged representation of who he is. It's the mask a man wears to protect himself and cover up his inner deficiencies.

Inferiority and the lack of light to reveal what a real man is supposed to be cause a man to settle and choose the mask to cover up his true self.

So why would a man need to cover himself and project a false image in the first place? It is because he feels inferior. Inferiority and the lack of light to reveal what a real man is supposed to be cause a man to settle and choose the mask to cover up his true self. He believes the mask will make him more accepted by others. I hope you can clearly see the progression. If not, the progression looks something like this.

Lack of Identity → Inferiority → Hiding

Like Adam, the fabricated man feels the need to cover himself. However, the fig leaves in our time represent any crutch a man relies on to cover up what he deems is his weakness. Unfortunately, we live in an age in which we've perfected phoniness—in which men would rather project strength they don't truly have.

Let me paint this picture to illustrate a point.

He's wearing his best suit. He spent time "pumping himself up." He looks in the mirror and sees his handsome reflection. He smiles. "You got this," he tells himself. Fear of rejection has no place in him. He's got his game face on. He's attending a dinner party with some very influential people who could take his business endeavor to the next level. He's rehearsed the outcome in his mind for weeks. He's even planned the light jokes he will tell over dinner. He's told his girlfriend she has to look "perfect" by his side tonight. He tries to ignore the accelerated pace of his heartbeat. He can't. He continues to look in the mirror. He tells himself he's not nervous. It's only the adrenaline flowing through his entire being—like a lion just before he makes the kill…at least that's what he tells himself. He takes one last look to reassure himself. Then he steps out to seize his destiny.

It's the end of the night. The outcome proved the anxiety he was feeling earlier to have been ill-founded. They loved him. He was professional, knowledgeable… and oh so charming. They even loved his girlfriend. He felt even prouder because she looked like the perfect trophy on his arm. They laughed at his jokes. Once he got in his zone, he felt as if he was soaring…playing to a sold-out crowd . . . and he received a standing ovation. It was a job well done.

Or was it? On the surface everything looks great. What his clients don't know is that although our hero is very talented at what he does in business, there is more beneath the surface. What they don't know is, he has been dating the beautiful woman on his arm for six years with no sign of commitment. Yet, he has taken her time, emotions, and even her body on more than one occasion. The clients also don't know that beneath all the charm and confident swagger lies a fearfully driven man. Much of his outward success is built on a foundation of fear about what would happen if he didn't succeed. They also don't know that he struggles with a nagging sense of boredom that causes him to watch pornography on an increasingly consistent basis, when he isn't busy building his business. And it doesn't stop there . . . he is actually one step from losing it all, which he is completely unaware of.

The above scenario is not every man's story; however, I wanted to paint a clear picture of the difference between the image that is portrayed and what is actually real. On the surface, a man can appear to be a real man. He can appear capable and strong, but that is what is projected in order to cover up the inner weaknesses that cause the most torment in his life. These "fig leaves" have been carefully chosen and constructed to cover up the real man who exists beneath the surface. He's a false fabrication and very far from what he really could be, from God's perspective. So, for the fabricated man, what are the consequences? Let's look at a few.

Burying the Genuine Man

A man who insists on wearing a mask and projecting a fabricated image of himself will never evolve into his most genuine self. Fear won't allow him to take that risk. As a result, he won't discover the value of who he really is. He plays it safe and only reveals what he thinks will make him most liked and revered among people, but that's not what the world needs. The world needs men who are genuine and not afraid to allow the fullness of who they are to shine. Besides, God wants you to reveal the real you. Look at Isaiah 62:2, 3 in the New Living Translation.

A man who insists on wearing a mask and projecting a fabricated image of himself will never evolve into his most genuine self.

"The nations will see your righteousness. World leaders will be blinded by your glory. And you will be given a new name by the Lord's own mouth. The Lord will hold you in his hand for all to see—a splendid crown in the hand of God."

In these scriptures, it seems to me that God wants to show you off! It is in our human nature to show off things that we value and are proud of. Likewise, God wants to do the same where you are concerned. Sadly, very few men choose God's way, so He cannot show them off. They are in hiding, and the real man is never seen, or is seen in mere glimpses. God wants you to take the mask off and allow Him to reveal the real you.

Character vs. Charm

Another reason a man constructs a false projection of himself is that he lacks character. In other words, a fabrication is needed only when a man lacks true substance of character. I like to define character as doing what's right because it's right and then doing it right. Your character is who you truly are when no one is looking. It's what you default to the most. Your character is based on your life's habits. Character is not something that can be faked. Further, character *is* the real man. When a man has a less than virtuous character, he will have to add charm to his repertoire. Charm is what you are for the moment. Character is who you are all the time.

Charm is what you are for the moment.
Character is who you are all the time.

"Every man's way is right in his own eyes, but the LORD weighs the hearts" (Proverbs 21:2 NASB).

This scripture gives insight into what matters most to God. He looks at the heart of man. Why? Man's character comes from his center. Many men are worn out because they are attempting to maintain a charming façade that does not reflect their true inner image. All the while, they are fearful that others will see that their outward display doesn't match their inner reality. This is a stressful way to live, and cannot be sustained indefinitely.

People often ask me, "Tell me...what's the different between Creflo Dollar the preacher and Creflo Dollar the man?" I always have the same response. There is no difference. I'm the same guy. The person you see in the pulpit is the same one you'll see at home with my family—flaws and all. It is this very trait that God used to propel me into ministry. I found that people were hungry for someone who told the truth and was not afraid to show who he really was. In my sermons, I reveal all my mistakes and blunders, not just my successes. They are all a part of what makes me who I am today. For example, people who have heard my sermons over the years have heard about my struggles with food—particularly apple pie. I've also talked about overcoming my issues with anger and my growth in the love of God.

You see, God is not looking for flawless men. He's looking for available men—men who are willing to answer His call. Regarding any shortcomings you have, God will make up the difference, so there's no need to hide behind a fabricated mask.

When It All Unravels

So what happens to the man who continues to project a false image? He continues to hide and only show people what he wants them to see. He refuses to deal with his internal issues, and the inevitable always happens—eventually it all comes crashing down. It has to, because it was never real in the first place.

Men who try to appear to be prosperous find themselves in this predicament. But lasting prosperity is not found in what you can purchase. Lasting prosperity is found in the character you develop. Eventually the "swagger" men try to reflect crumbles, because God will not allow a man to avoid facing his character deficiencies. God loves us. Therefore, He will do whatever it takes to see every man healed and whole. That is why the path of the fabricated man always ends in shame and disillusionment.

Lasting prosperity is found in the character you develop.

If you are living the life of the fabricated man, you can change. Begin by being honest with yourself and God. This will require courage. Unfortunately, you would be surprised to know how few men there are who find the courage to change. Don't let that be true of you. Matthew 23:25, 26 shows us how strong Jesus' conviction was about living outward demonstrations that don't reflect who we really are on the inside. It reads:

Hypocrites! For you are so careful to clean the outside of the cup and the dish, but inside you are filthy . . . First wash the inside . . . and then the outside will become clean, too.

Take Jesus' word for it. Get the inside right first, then work on the outside, because a time will come when you won't be able to cover up anymore. Your success as a man depends on it.

A man that has the courage to change doesn't need to hide behind a mask.

God has a day of visitation planned in the life of every man. The day of visitation is the day when the thing you've hoped, worked, and believed for comes to pass suddenly. It's when God manifests Himself in your circumstance in a tangible way. The problem is He is unable to do this fully if you are out of position. So if things seem dry in your life, it's not that the faucet is turned off. You're just in the wrong location. A man who has the courage to change doesn't need to hide behind a mask. Change your position by aligning your thoughts about your life with God's Word. Then you will know for yourself that God's Word is real, and you will have the fruit to show for it.

4

MALE VS. MAN

Scornful men bring a city into a snare: but wise men turn away wrath.

—PROVERBS 29:8

But thou, O man of God, flee these things; and follow after righteousness, godliness, faith, love, patience, meekness.

—1 TIMOTHY 6:11

Seest thou a man diligent in his business? he shall stand before kings; he shall not stand before mean men.

—PROVERBS 22:29

Manhood is not guaranteed. It's not an automatic thing, and it doesn't come with age. Real manhood is something that must be developed one decision at a time. In other words, manhood is a choice.

This may be a hard statement to swallow, but it is important that you understand there is a difference between being a male and being a man. One is by nature, and the other is by choice. Yet most people believe manhood is automatic. While you were born into this world a male, and have the physical equipment that identifies you as a male, that doesn't mean you will automatically become a man at a certain age.

Manhood goes far beyond a male's physical externalities.

We've all heard the cliché, "Having the ability to make a baby doesn't make you a man; being able to raise the baby makes you a man." I totally agree with this statement. Manhood goes far beyond a male's physical externalities. Furthermore, males are animalistic in nature. We are governed by what we feel and our natural senses. We are not driven by logic, principles, or governing morality. Instead, we are driven by natural instinct and tendencies. I liken males to pieces of clay—all raw materials without the sculpting, polishing, and development.

Have you ever heard men make this statement: "Well, I'm just a man…what do you expect from me?" This is usually the comment made when they make excuses for not being able to control their animalistic urges, particularly where sex is concerned. I'd like to add clarity. Males who think this way are not operating in real manhood at all. They are simply operating carnally as undeveloped males who merely have the potential to be men. There is a very familiar scripture in the Bible that sheds light on this. "When I was a child, I spake as a child, I understood as a child, I thought as a child: but when I became a man, I put away childish things" (1 Corinthians 13:11).

The Apostle Paul is speaking in this scripture, and notice he did not say he became a man when he got older or merely grew out of childhood. It doesn't work that way from God's perspective. The scripture says he *became* a man. The word *became* implies that something must happen to initiate the change.

What has to happen? All childish things must be put away if we are going to become real men.

In other words, a decision has to be made. If this decision is never made, then it is possible for a boy to live his entire life and get older in age but never become a man. I've met males who were older but were still very much entrenched in childish things.

Manhood is more than maleness.

Manhood is more than maleness. Maleness deals with nature and manhood deals with purpose. Without understanding the purpose of manhood, all we're left with are males who are void of the true essence of what real manhood is all about. Remember, in Genesis God created male and female to reflect His image (Genesis 1:27). But it wasn't until God breathed into his nostrils and put His Spirit on the inside of the male that he became what he was meant to be. This lets us know that you're not a man until God enters your spirit. God didn't intend for you to be born a male and remain there. He expects each man to take the next step: to be born again and filled with His Spirit.

God has left this choice up to us. He will not make the choice for us. Yet He has made it clear regarding the outcome for every male who does not choose His road to manhood. "I call heaven and earth to record this day against you, that I have set before you life and death, blessing and cursing: therefore choose life, that both thou and thy seed may live" (Deuteronomy 30:19).

Without God it's impossible to be anything other than just a male who's subject to carnality. You'll be governed by animal instincts. What does an animal do? Animals do everything by instinct, without thought or reason. It's what they are wired to do, and that's all they know to do. This is true of men who are hardwired toward the things of the flesh versus the things of the spirit. They have multiple sex partners because they feel like it. They are dominated by cravings and urges. Further, the actions of these men are motivated by their feelings, which will always lead them down the wrong path. Since their thoughts and feelings are not aligned with God's Word, they will never reach the right destination.

Should a man in this condition gain some good information and attempt to go in the right direction, eventually his old nature and wrong instincts will resurface, leading back in the wrong direction. Why? A man cannot evolve from being a male into manhood in his own power. He needs God.

A man cannot evolve from being a male into manhood in his own power. He needs God.

To get to the root of it all, I like what author John Eldridge said, "True manhood is spiritual." I love that. It could not be more simply stated. True manhood in its very essence is spiritual. As such, I understand why so many men are not living God's true purpose for their lives. They have not made the connection that our manhood is tied to our spirituality in God. We've seen our manhood as tied to our bank account, the adequacy of the equipment between our legs, how women view us, our accomplishments or lack thereof, and so on. But we have not tied our masculinity and manhood to our connection and relationship with God.

Jesus said in John 6:63, "The words that I speak unto you, they are spirit."

This means the source of all spirituality comes from what Jesus has said. What makes a man spiritual is his relationship with the Word of God. I know this is not a popular view. Our society thinks the Bible is an outdated fable. The sad reality is only few men will grasp the truth. However, there will come a time when it will be obvious who the real men are. God will personally see to that.

> *If you don't have the Word in your life—*
> *reading it daily and allowing it to govern*
> *your life—your potential for manhood is*
> *severely limited.*

If you don't have the Word in your life—reading it daily and allowing it to govern your life—your potential for manhood is severely limited. You will be stuck in maleness for the rest of your life with a warped or incomplete definition of manhood, because you can't define manhood without God.

Key Symptoms of Maleness

A Male Lacks Responsibility

Winston Churchill said, "The price of greatness is responsibility." We will never be great men if we do not accept responsibility for our lives. I have counseled men who like to talk about how life "happened to them," but life doesn't just happen. Life is a result of what goes on inside us. Life comes out of us. The matrix in our center is what produces our lives as men.

Keep thy heart with all diligence; for out of it are the issues of life.

(PROVERBS 4:23)

God has made us responsible for our issues in life. Whatever gets in us is what we will find coming out of us, and what comes out of us is responsible for the life we currently have. Men spend great amounts of energy battling outward circumstances. However, this is not God's method. God wants you to take responsibility for the root of the matter. We cannot play the blame game as Adam did. We can't blame God. We can't even blame the devil. Wherever we currently find ourselves in life is a result of our past choices.

Please don't get me wrong. I am not saying you haven't had things come against you in life. You may have been born into challenging circumstances. However, God doesn't want you to use that as an excuse to remain the same. I love what author Brian Tracy said: "The happiest people in the world are those who feel absolutely terrific about themselves, and this is the natural outgrowth of accepting total responsibility for every part of their lives."

*Look at a sad and depressed man and
I guarantee you are looking at a man who
hasn't taken responsibility for what he
can do to make his life better.*

Look at a sad and depressed man and I guarantee you are looking at a man who hasn't taken responsibility for what he can do to make his life better. Even when terrible things happen to us, we still must take responsibility for the outcome. Let me give you an example. I remember when my father died. I was at the movies with my daughter when I received a call to come to the hospital. I rushed to the hospital to meet my family. However, by the time I got there, Daddy was gone. Such an intense pain hit me internally. We were finally developing a deeper relationship, and now he was gone. I didn't get a chance to say good-bye. I felt as though my arm had been ripped off.

At that point, I had a decision to make. My emotions were telling me to stop preaching and take a break from the ministry. Although I was really in a lot of pain, I knew God was counting on me to continue the work He had called me to do. So through my tears and pain, I decided to keep teaching the

Word of God. As a result of taking on the responsibility to control the pain I was feeling and trusting God to heal me, I was propelled further down the road toward His vision for my life.

All of us have crossroads in our lives. However, we must respond in a way that will take us to our desired destination, and refuse to make excuses. Further, when we fail to accept complete responsibility for the condition of our lives, nothing will work. We will remain out of control and incapable of change. Sadly, we will be sentenced to a life of running like mad, yet remaining in the same place.

You must properly manage your spirit, soul, and physical body.

Please accept this truth: You are responsible for managing your life. Management begins with your spirit. You must properly manage your spirit, soul, and physical body. Ultimately, that translates into proper management of your entire life. When that occurs, God will be pleased with you, and you will be pleased with the positive outcome of your life.

A Male Lacks Foresight

One of biggest detriments to walking in real manhood is when a male is driven by improper impulses that cause him to operate without foresight. Foresight is simply the ability to look ahead and plan for the future. A male only lives for today. He's not thinking of what may come tomorrow. So he wastes his most valuable asset—his time—while living for the moment. He's too busy enjoying the pleasures of living apart from God, unaware that the pleasures of sin only last for a season (Hebrews 11:25). Once you reach the end of the course, the only thing left is to face the consequences. However, maleness doesn't allow him to look that far ahead. The only thing it will afford this man is the ability to live in regret because he didn't change sooner.

A great man knows that if he's connected to God, he can be prepared for the future.

A great man knows that if he's connected to God, he can be prepared for the future. This kind of man is not willing to jeopardize his future for the sake of present impulses to live in a way that disagrees with what's right, regardless of how appealing it may feel or seem at the moment.

A Male Can't Commit to Anything

A man is a finisher. Anyone can start something great. But people don't remember how you start. People only remember how you finish. What separates the male who starts from the man who finishes? One word. Commitment. A man is committed to God and the course He has planned for his life. Males who have yet to grasp their manhood are falling away in record numbers from their marriages and other important areas of life. A real man knows, regardless of whether times are good or bad, he doesn't change the commitment he's made. It takes true depth of character to do this. Anyone can be committed when things are going well, but a man is also committed during times of controversy, tests, and trials.

Well done, thou good and faithful servant: thou hast been faithful over a few things, I will make thee ruler over many things: enter thou into the joy of thy lord.

(MATTHEW 25:21)

Real men strive to hear Jesus utter those words. They are counted among the faithful who are committed to doing what God last told them to do. These men will press through disappointment, failure, attacks, being misunderstood, and long seasons when things appear not to be working. However, males will get picked off along the way. They may start out great, but you never see them reach the end of the course. On the other hand, real men finish. You will finish, too. The mere fact that you are reading this book denotes your sincere desire to fulfill your destiny. Just remain committed, not in your strength but in the strength of the Lord. If you do, you will evolve into the man you dream of becoming.

A Male's Sexuality Is Perverted

A book about men for men would not be complete without addressing this issue. I will attack this from a different angle later on, but up front, let me say this: A male is unaware of God's purpose for sex and sexuality. A male's view of sex is strictly selfish—it invigorates him and is for his pleasure only. In our present society, the purity of sex has been brutalized. From pornography to music videos and movies, males everywhere are driven to all kinds of sexual sin (masturbation, oral sex, adultery, and so on) that will inevitably keep a male from reaching his status as a man.

> *God's will is for you to be holy, so stay away from all sexual sin. Then each of you will control his own body and live in holiness and honor—not in lustful passion like the pagans who do not know God and his ways.*
>
> (1 THESSALONIANS 4:3–5 NLT)

Real men know how to honor God in their bodies and sexual lives by not engaging in sexual activities outside of marriage.

This scripture is pretty clear regarding God's instruction on how we are to carry ourselves. Real men know how to honor God in their bodies and sexual lives by not engaging in sexual activities outside of marriage. All sexual activity outside of the covenant of marriage is selfish in its origin and will surely cause us to suffer in our development as men.

Sadly, there are males who will choose to ignore God's instruction and go on with their current lifestyle because it "feels good." The Bible warns us about what happens to men who participate in sexual sin and perversion.

> *...as a result of this sin, they suffered within themselves the penalty they deserved.*
>
> (ROMANS 1:27 NLT)

I urge you to allow the Word of God to be your final authority regarding your sex life. Through His Word, God will show you how wonderful sex can be in the confines of marriage, but you won't discover that doing it the world's way. Become a man who can grasp this truth and live by it.

A Male Has No Relationship with God

I believe this last point is critical. You may know some very good men who have wonderful traits. Many of them may even be responsible to a certain degree. They take good care of their families and make good role models. Personally, I know men like this who really have it together. As such, it may appear that what I'm talking about doesn't apply to them. Well, that depends.

I believe males who possess these positive traits are on the right path to real manhood. But in God's view, they are still lacking. He made it clear in His Word that all our good works are as filthy rags before His sight (Isaiah 64:6).

God is perfect. *So even at your best, if you are not in Him, you are flawed.*

God is perfect. So even at your best, if you are not in Him, you are flawed. Therefore, unless a male is born again in Jesus Christ, *he will never become a real man.* He is stuck in maleness and the curse of sin, which was released in the garden when the first man decided to take off manhood and yield to the devil. Choose to disconnect from the failure of maleness, and receive victory through Jesus, which will empower you to walk in true manhood.

5

THE "IT'S ALL ABOUT ME" MAN

It is not good to eat much honey: so for men
to search their own glory is not glory.

—PROVERBS 25:27

Watch ye, stand fast in the faith, quit
you like men, be strong. Let all your
things be done with charity.

—1 CORINTHIANS 16:13–14

Iron sharpeneth iron; so a man sharpeneth
the countenance of his friend.

—PROVERBS 27:17

*T*he "It's all about Me" man can never be a real man. *A man cannot be happy when he can't see anything beyond himself.*

There is a character flaw in all of us that can easily become a weakness if we are conditioned to submit to it. This character flaw can be summed up in one word: *selfishness.* Selfishness is something a man must conquer before he can become a *real* man. Unfortunately, like a cancer, selfishness can dwell in him for years without detection while sapping his strength and causing a host of other problems as well. Therefore, when a man becomes serious about reaching the peak stature of manhood, he will uncover, expose, and deal with selfishness.

Selfishness is something a man must conquer before he can become a **real** *man.*

The dictionary defines a selfish person as *one who is devoted to or caring chiefly for oneself, or one who is concerned primarily with one's own interests, benefits, and welfare, regardless of others.* When we read a harsh definition like this one, our tendency is to defend ourselves by saying, "Well, I may have some selfish ways, but I'm not that bad. I'm not mainly concerned with myself."

Let's look at this from God's perspective. Remember, God's view is very different from our point of reference. Usually we make comparisons with other people. We think, *Well, I'm not as bad as that guy.* Although you may not be as selfish as the next man, the fact that there are traces of it in your life opens the door for you to be destroyed from the inside out.

The issue of selfishness has its origin in the Garden of Eden. Adam was created by God for relationship and fellowship. Before Eve came along, all of Adam's time was spent in fellowship with God. He was conscious of and surrounded by God and His presence. That was all Adam knew.

The issue of selfishness has its origin in the Garden of Eden.

The devil knew as long as Adam was focused on God, His presence, and His Word he was literally invincible. So what ploy did Satan use? He got Adam and Eve to take their focus off of God and turn it toward themselves. This is what he also attempts to do in your life. He'll tell you God is holding out on you. He'll show you how desirable "the fruit" is and urge you to take a bite. All the while, you begin to become increasingly more aware of yourself and what you think are the benefits you will gain, as you become less aware of God.

We were born into a world that tells us over and over, "Look out for yourself."

We were born into a world that tells us over and over, "Look out for yourself." In addition, the pains and wounds we suffer as young boys and throughout life tend to make us believe this is how we ought to be. Experiences such as a parent abandoning the family, rejection by a woman, and unaccomplished dreams can leave a man with a void that no amount of success can fill. He therefore becomes stuck, constantly striving to reach the next plateau in hopes of acquiring the peace he longs to have. In the midst of these difficult situations, these messages are playing over and over in his mind:

Look out for yourself.

No one is looking out for you. You have to do it all by yourself.

If you aren't concerned about you... who else will be?

The problem is, many young boys have never been told that they were not created to take care of themselves. We were created to be dependent on, not independent of, God. Here are a few scriptures to support this statement:

Acts 17:28 says, "For in him we live, and move, and have our being... For we are also his offspring."

"The Lord is the strength of my life" (Psalm 27:1).

"My eyes are always on the Lord, for he rescues me from the traps of my enemies" (Psalm 25:15 NLT).

The strongest man is nothing without the strength of God.

The strongest man is nothing without the strength of God.

Selfishness is the cornerstone in the life of a man who doesn't know that God is his only source. Sadly, he is unaware that God has his back. So he makes himself the chief concern of his life. However, a man, in and of himself, has limited resources. Jesus knew this truth. He lived in desperate dependence on God. Jesus said, "I can of mine own self do nothing" (John 5:30). He knew God was His source. Therefore, Jesus wasn't concerned about Himself. As a result, He exhibited power unlike anything the world had ever seen. Therefore, selfishness always limits the flow of power in a man. Adam is an example of this. He was powerful before he became totally focused on himself. As soon as he got into selfishness and sin, Adam was completely uncovered, cowering in shame.

Second Timothy 3:1, 2 states: "This know also, that in the last days perilous times shall come. For men shall be lovers of their own selves." These verses describe the present condition of our society, and the root issue.

---

*We are living in a world where people are
chiefly lovers of themselves.*

The Amplified Bible translates perilous times as *times of great stress and trouble that are hard to deal with and hard to bear.* Why is the world threatened by terrorism, recessions, disasters, crime, and so on? Why are men faced with such trying times that will cause them to wonder if they can bear it? The answer is clear. We are living in a world where people are chiefly lovers of themselves. Being preoccupied with self all the time can create a lot of stress.

The only outlets for a selfish man are vain amusements and selfish pleasures. Show me an addicted man, and I'll show you a selfish man. His desire for selfish gratification has taken over because it is his only outlet and release from the cares of his life. The issues of life and suggestions of Satan will make sure a selfish man is confronted every day with things that will keep him concerned about his life. This is why it's critical for a man—particularly a man who has a wife and children—to know he's cared for and taken care of by God. There is simply no other antidote for selfishness and the anxiety that comes with it.

Jesus paints a crystal clear illustration of this in Matthew chapter 6 in the New Living Bible. "No one can serve two masters. For you will hate one and love the other; you will be devoted to one and despise the other. You cannot serve both God and money."

It is important to point out that a man who doesn't recognize God as his only source is a slave to money. But it doesn't have to be this way. God doesn't have a problem with our having money. In fact, it is one of the most basic provisions from God. But a man who has selfishly and foolishly made himself his own source will eventually make money his master.

It is important to point out that a man who doesn't recognize God as his only source is a slave to money.

Matthew 6:30–33 in the New Living Translation says:

God will certainly care for you. Why do you have so little faith? So don't worry about these things, saying, "What will we eat? What will we drink? What will we wear?" These things dominate the thoughts of unbelievers, but your heavenly Father already knows all your needs. Seek the Kingdom of God above all else, and live righteously, and he will give you everything you need.

The key to getting out of selfishness is realizing that God will take care of all your needs. Yes, you are a man. Yes, you are supposed to lead. Yes, you are meant to be strong and a reflection of God's glory in the earth. But you were not created to be your own source. Neither are other things and people meant to be your source. However, selfishness will drive you to every poor substitute for the real thing.

The key to getting out of selfishness is realizing that God will take care of all your needs.

After reading these scriptures, you still may not be completely convinced that selfishness is harmful to your development into real manhood. This scripture should remove all doubt: "If you follow your selfish desires, you will harvest destruction, but if you follow the Spirit, you will harvest eternal life" (Galatians 6:8 CEV).

If you follow after selfishness you are following the path that leads to death.

I can recall when God spoke to me about selfishness in my life. He said something I will never forget. "Selfishness is the root cause of all lack a man will experience in his life."

We saw this truth in Adam's life. As soon as he fell into selfishness and sin, he experienced the curse, and lack showed up in his life as a result of being driven from the Garden of Eden—his place of excess and abundance. Adam knew no lack until sin, which was birthed from a foundation of selfishness, showed up in his life.

---

*Adam knew no lack until sin, which was
birthed from a foundation of selfishness,
showed up in his life.*

Look at your own life. For example, if you are married, is your marriage plagued with strife and disharmony? If so, selfishness is at the root of your unhappy marriage. Or, are you struggling with anxiety about your life, and you lack peace? If so, you have probably crowned yourself as your own god and have cornered yourself into a place of self-centeredness.

Selfishness is the opposite of love. It is also the foundation upon which Satan operates. The good news is Jesus came to free us from the law of sin and death, which is selfishness. God loves us and is intimately aware of everything concerning us. He knew us before we were born, and He has a good plan for our lives (Jeremiah 29:11). He simply wants us to trust in the fact that He has already made provision to take care of us. When we receive this truth, we can rest. And the need to be focused on ourselves will disappear.

The Power of God-Consciousness

Before you came into relationship with Jesus, you were most likely trained to live as if God didn't exist. However, if you are ever going to get rid of selfishness, you must develop a God-consciousness. In other words, you must come to a point in your life where you realize God is not some vague, distant mist or cloud. He is a person. He is more real than the problems you are currently experiencing, which are temporary. God's love and His Word are eternal (Romans 8:18). While your problems are temporary, God's answers are everlasting. Your trial has an expiration date, but there is no limit to God's promises to you!

God gave us the free will to choose life or death.

God gave us the free will to choose life or death. We can choose to grow in fellowship and relationship with God or not. Please understand that we can't do both. We will either fellowship and grow in God, or we will remain focused on and in fellowship with our problems.

"Who shall separate us from the love of Christ? shall tribulation, or distress, or persecution, or famine, or nakedness, or peril, or sword?...Nay, in all these things we are more than conquerors through him that loved us" (Romans 8:35, 37).

Please pay special attention to the last line of this scripture. God's will for your life is for you to be *more* than a conqueror. A conqueror is someone who wins battles consistently. As you become more conscious of God and His unlimited power working on your behalf, you become more than a conqueror!

I don't know about you, but scriptures like Romans 8:35, 37 create a sense of invincibility in me. I realize I don't have to carry the weight of this world on my shoulders. God, who loves me, upholds me. The number one thing that will make you a man who's more than a conqueror is your complete confidence in God's love for you. When your mind is anchored in this truth, you'll rest in God's love, knowing everything that concerns you is in His capable hands. As a result, you will think less and less of yourself because you are no longer your own source.

The number one thing that will make you a man who's more than a conqueror is your complete confidence in God's love for you.

This growth will take you to the peak of manhood as you become more focused on what you can give rather than on what you can receive. Nothing eradicates selfishness more than acts of giving that are motivated by love. However, you can only achieve this kind of lifestyle by first being convinced that you do not have to be overly concerned about your life. This is the first step in the progression toward freedom.

Finally, your life was never meant to be just about you. God's calling on your life is an adventure that is meant to take you beyond yourself. Since God already has you covered, you are free to offer up your life as a gift to make this world a better place for someone else.

God's calling on your life is an adventure that is meant to take you beyond yourself.

It is my prayer that you will begin today to eradicate any traces of selfishness in your life. By trusting in God's Word and applying it to your life, you will become empowered to focus on God and all that He has equipped you to do for His Kingdom. As you continue to serve others, it will become more about others and less about you, allowing you to grow and develop into the man God has created and destined you to be.

6

THE FEAR FACTOR

Have not I commanded thee? Be strong and of a good courage; be not afraid, neither be thou dismayed: for the Lord thy God is with thee whithersoever thou goest.

—JOSHUA 1:9

When I was a child, I spake as a child, I understood as a child, I thought as a child: but when I became a man, I put away childish things.

—1 CORINTHIANS 13:11

Fear is our greatest enemy. It keeps us from soaring, and it keeps us bound and shackled. Although God created us to be free, we can never fully experience our freedom until we deal with the thing we fear the most, and laugh in its face.

Many years ago, I was in a very intense counseling session with a gentleman. After a few hours had passed, it appeared as if we were making very little progress. This guy had a successful business and was very wealthy, but he was on his second marriage, which was failing. It was obvious he was suffering from symptoms of depression. Spiritually he was like an unwatered garden, as he was facing a spiritual drought in every sense of the word.

Yet, as he continued to talk to me, he maintained an air of defiant pride. I wondered why he was in my office for counseling if he only wanted to talk and give *reasons* for why he should remain the same. As he went on and on, the Spirit of God whispered something so simple and clear to me. *"Ask him what is he afraid of."*

As he went on and on, the Spirit of God
whispered something so simple and clear to
me. "Ask him what is he afraid of."

The question was so clear it cut through me like a knife. Instantly I saw it. Everything we had talked about was merely dealing with the "fruit" issues in his life, but we hadn't exposed the *root* of his issues.

I quickly interrupted his ramblings and asked him what he was afraid of. I didn't really know what to expect. I simply watched him as the color seemed to drain out of his face. He tried to speak, but it seemed as if the air had been knocked out of him. Then, without his speaking a word, an uncontrollable flood of tears and sobs erupted from him. With his head in his hands, I knew we had hit a gusher. I'll never forget his answer. *"EVERYTHING!"*

I was stunned. Everything? The question had caught him off guard and at the same time opened the floodgates. What followed was an overflow of revealed honesty concerning fear of measuring up to his father's standard. He was driven by fear to be successful and not be looked upon as a failure. But the more successful he became the more his fear of failing grew. It was this fear that drove him and cost him his first marriage and was quickly causing the deterioration of his second one. The resulting depression was simply the fruit of feeling the fear that all the success he had built would someday come crashing down.

It was this fear that drove him and cost him his first marriage and was quickly causing the deterioration of his second one.

In all honesty, it was a breakthrough for me as much as it was for him. Up until this time I understood what the Bible had to say about fear. God repeatedly commands us in His Word to *fear not*. This phrase and its variations appear well over three hundred times throughout the Bible. It's the paramount command from the Lord. FEAR NOT.

My breakthrough was receiving the revelation that fear is not just an *issue*. On the contrary, it is the root issue of all issues—anger, depression, addiction, adultery, insecurity, and so on can all be traced back to fear. This was a defining moment for me in ministry. I immediately began studying what the Word of God had to say about fear from a fresh perspective. And now I want you to benefit from what years of counseling, study, and even dealing with it in my own life have taught me. I want you to be free, too.

*My breakthrough was receiving the revelation
that fear is not just an* issue.

Ralph Waldo Emerson said, "Fear defeats more people than any other thing in the world." I believe that is a true statement. I've encountered many men who seemed unable to get a grasp of how dangerous fear is, let alone conquer it in their lives. But if you are going to be God's man, you're going to have to face it and defeat it by realizing that God has already provided the means for you to live free from fear.

Fear not...

Be not afraid...

Thou shalt not fear...

These are paramount orders to the man who is a true warrior in the army of the Lord. And it is just that—an army. When you chose to enter a personal relationship with Jesus you also enlisted in His army. God is a warrior. The Bible refers to Him as "The Man of War" (Exodus 15:3). He fully expects every man to be His warrior and use His power to confront darkness wherever he encounters it. This is exactly what Jesus did. Everywhere He went He boldly confronted the work of the devil and set people free. If we are going to do what Jesus did, it is critical to eradicate fear from our lives.

*When you chose to enter a personal
relationship with Jesus you also enlisted
in His army.*

Jesus knew, due to Adam's sin in the garden, every man is susceptible to the fear of death, which is the master fear of all fears. However, He came to deliver us from fear. Hebrews 2:15 says: "And deliver them who through fear of death were all their lifetime subject to bondage." It is through this fear and all of its many other forms that men are brought into slavery. Far too many men have no idea that they are in bondage to the devil through fear. Furthermore, there is no amount of money, success, fame, or anything in this physical realm capable of setting us free from the bondage of fear. Only our complete trust in Jesus will deliver us from the bondage of fear.

*Far too many men have no idea that they are
in bondage to the devil through fear.*

We live in a world in which the fearless reign and the fearful live as slaves. Fear is a thief and a robber. It robs great men of their great destinies. It holds kings captive. The man who conquers in life is fearless. He is the man who gives no place to fear. Fearlessness gives conquerors backbone for great exploits and achievements.

Many men think the Bible is outdated. As a result, they don't really see a need for all this "Jesus stuff." Many of them find it easy to live their entire lives without Jesus; however, when they are lying on their deathbeds they are faced with the fear of not knowing what's going to happen to them. Desperately, they call on Jesus to deliver them. Fortunately, Jesus, in His love and grace, meets them right there and delivers them. But it doesn't have to be that way for us. God desires for us to live in victory *now*.

Fear Defined

If we are going to be free from fear and live as conquerors then we must know what fear is. I want to approach this from two aspects—from the natural and spiritual—so you can get a clear understanding. God ordered the universe to be governed by laws—natural and spiritual laws. A law is simply an established principle that works all the time for whoever chooses to operate it. For example, in the natural realm, gravity is a law that works the same for everyone who gets involved in it. There is no prejudice. Anyone who steps off the side of a building will plummet to the ground. Why? Gravity is a law that works all the time. On the other hand, the Bible is simply the law of the spiritual realm.

If we are going to be free from fear and live as conquerors then we must know what fear is.

Faith and fear are laws, and they both operate by faith. They work all the time for whoever chooses to get involved in them. One of them operates by faith going in the positive direction, the other one operates by faith going in the negative direction. When your faith goes in a negative direction it becomes contaminated and it's called fear.

Faith and fear are two sides of the same coin. They both operate by the same principle. Faith will pull from the unseen spiritual realm the thing from God you want and believe for. Fear is simply a reciprocal of faith, and it will pull from the unseen realm the thing from the devil you don't want but you believe. In order to be in fear you have to believe something that opposes what God has promised in His Word.

Faith and fear are two sides of the same coin.
They both operate by the same principle.

Your enemy—the devil—knows that God established the universe on laws. So his tactic is to get us to activate the laws that lead to death, ultimately defeating ourselves. It is through fear that the enemy gains access and clearance into our lives. This is why we must know Jesus has already defeated the devil. But Satan counts on our ignorance of what God has said in His Word. Our lack of knowledge of the Word is the foundation by which all fear can thrive in our lives and destroy us.

"Be sober, be vigilant; because your adversary the devil, as a roaring lion, walketh about, seeking whom he may devour" (1 Peter 5:8). This is God's instruction to every man. Be alert. Be awake. Don't be ignorant. Why? You have an adversary—the devil. However, please look at a few key words in this verse. "As a roaring lion." We can all agree a lion is a ferocious animal. However, the devil is not a roaring lion. He only pretends to be one. Who is the lion? Jesus is called the Lion of Judah. He's the lion. He defeated the devil who is pretending to be more than he is.

However, the devil is not a roaring lion.
He only pretends to be one.

The other thing the scripture reveals is that the devil can't just devour anyone. He has to seek whom he can devour. He is limited in his ability. So who is he seeking to devour? He is looking for the man who hasn't conquered his fears. Fear is the devil's calling card and he feels welcome wherever it is present.

There is something I want to focus on in 1 Peter 5:7.

Casting all your care upon him; for he careth for you.

God wants us to cast every concern for our lives on Him. Man was never meant to be his own source. God is our only source. When we are self-driven and self-focused, we take on the cares of meeting our needs. As a result, this foundation of fear is constantly at work in our lives.

Fear is a spiritual connector. This truth is revealed in the story of Job. Many people are familiar with Job's story, but they may not fully be aware of what opened the door for the enemy to come in and destroy his life. The answer is found in Job 3:25.

For the thing which I greatly feared is come upon me, and that which I was afraid of is come unto me.

Job lost his family, his health, and his sanity because of fear. It connected him to the thing he feared. The enemy uses fear to kill, steal, and destroy us, while faith is the means by which the promises of God manifest in our lives. God hates fear because it prevents us from receiving His best. From His perspective, fear is something that cannot and should not be tolerated at all.

The enemy uses fear to kill, steal, and destroy us.

Furthermore, based on what happened to Adam in the garden, we should be convinced that no amount of fear is good. The first thing Adam expressed after falling from glory was how afraid he was. He was a fearless man before the fall. All he knew was God. But the minute selfishness and sin came in, fear immediately followed.

The world has a different perspective regarding fear. Have you ever heard someone say, "You know, a little fear can be good for you." I understand what people mean when they say that, but the reality of it is not true. No amount of fear is good. To say a little fear is good is to say a little of the devil is good. Or, a little sin is good.

I have seen examples of men in the world who have achieved great success whose testimony was, "I was afraid of being average" or "I was afraid of what would happen if I never did what I was created to do." Statements like this sound very noble. And because these people are very successful, it is easy to think that maybe fear does have some good aspects.

If fear motivates us to be successful, our souls will be tormented with the fear of losing everything we obtain. This is why God wants our faith in Him to be the motivating force behind all that we do. It's the only thing that will give us a sure foundation to build upon.

God wants our faith in Him to be the motivating force behind all that we do.

The Antidote for Fear

There are two fundamental truths I want you to understand if you are going to conquer fear. The first thing you must understand is *why you are afraid.* Fear doesn't just happen. There's a reason it gains access in your life. When a man is afraid he's afraid because of what he anticipates could happen based on what he sees, hears, and feels. For instance, it looks as if you won't get the contract. It looks as if you are going to die from some horrible disease. It looks as if your wife is going to leave you. The enemy is counting on all the seemingly true evidence he lays before you to convince you that your fears are real.

When we are confronted with things that are tempting us to fear the possibility of a negative outcome, we must decide to go to a higher source for our information. God is that source. His Word has a promise for every area of life. Whatever we are dealing with, God has an answer for that problem. Fear comes in when we feel incapable of dealing with the challenge. But remember, God is our source. He wants us to trust Him to deal with the things that concern us the most.

It is the presence of God. Being in His presence frees us from fear.

The second antidote is something very few men have tapped into, but it is indispensable if we are going to live free from fear. It is the presence of God. Being in His presence frees us from fear. Hebrews 13:5 and 6 in the Amplified Bible states:

> *[God] Himself has said, I will not in any way fail you nor give you up nor leave you without support. [I will] not, [I will] not, [I will] not in any degree leave you helpless nor forsake nor let [you] down (relax My hold on you)! [Assuredly not!]*
>
> *So we take comfort and are encouraged and confidently and boldly say, The Lord is my Helper; I will not be seized with alarm [I will not fear or dread or be terrified].*

No matter where you find yourself in life, no matter what mistakes you've made, no matter how bad it looks, God has never left nor will He ever leave you. This is a promise He is incapable of breaking, because He loves you. However, you must believe Jesus loves you. The man who believes in God's love becomes invulnerable to fear.

God loves us no matter what. Yet many men struggle to receive His love. They are convinced that their sin has caused God to stop loving them. There is nothing we can do that will ever cause God to stop loving us. Jesus died and shed His blood for our sins, so that God could have us all to Himself again.

When God looks at born-again men, He's not looking at our sins or our efforts to try to be right before Him. He is looking at us through Jesus' perfection. When we rest in the finished perfection of Jesus' sinless life, then fear and guilt will never be able to convince us that God doesn't love us. Men who are rooted in God's love have no problem receiving God's provision. God is with us always. Therefore, we can face every enemy and boldly declare "Jesus loves me and He is with me." No foe we will ever face has an answer for that.

God loves us no matter what. Yet many
men struggle to receive His love.

I have given you the antidote to eradicate fear from your life forever. Use it and be free!

7

THE UNHOLY TRINITY

Wise men lay up knowledge: but the mouth of the foolish is near destruction.

—PROVERBS 10:14

Blessed is the man that walketh not in the counsel of the ungodly, nor standeth in the way of sinners, nor sitteth in the seat of the scornful.

—PSALM 1:1

But I would have you know, that the head of every man is Christ; and the head of the woman [is] the man; and the head of Christ [is] God.

—1 CORINTHIANS 11:3

When it comes to the challenges that face us, we have to come to terms with the fact that there is an "unholy trinity," the world, the flesh, and the devil, that is constantly working to trip us up in our daily walk with God. The good news is that we have been empowered with the ability to overcome this three-fold system of attack when we release our faith in what Jesus has done for us. You must keep in mind that you are, first and foremost, a spiritual being who possesses a soul (mind, will, and emotions) and lives in a physical body. When you became born again, your spirit is re-created in righteousness and true holiness, and is identical to Jesus Christ. However, your soul and your body are not re-created. You still have the same mind, will, and emotions you had before you got saved, and your body still has the same desires it had before salvation. These are the two areas that the enemy uses as targets for his attacks. This is why we must renew our minds on a daily basis so that our souls and bodies line up with the desires of our born-again spirits.

*This is why we must renew our minds on a
daily basis so that our souls and bodies line
up with the desires of our born-again spirits.*

As we explore the unholy trinity, it's important to define what we are talking about. First I want to deal with the "world." When the Scriptures talk about the "world" or something being "worldly" they are referring to a way of thinking and operating that goes against the Word of God. The world encompasses the fallen, spiritually bankrupt, and corrupt environment we live in, with all of its ideologies, secular humanist beliefs, and methods of operation that have nothing to do with God. The "world" is a system that is based on self-effort; it completely leaves God out of the equation and has no hope outside of the capabilities of man. It is a system that is rapidly falling apart, which is why it is futile to put your trust in it.

First John 2:15–17 gives us a very simple and clear picture of what constitutes the world and how we should look at it. In this passage of scripture the Apostle John is giving instructions to Believers. He says, "Love not the world, neither the things that are in the world. If any man love the world, the love of the Father is not in him. For all that is in the world, the lust of the flesh, and the lust of the eyes, and the pride of life, is not of the Father, but is of the world. And the world passeth away, and the lust thereof: but he that doeth the will of God abideth for ever."

The world system is in direct opposition to God and His Word.

The world system is in direct opposition to God and His Word. Everything about it can be summed up in the lust of the eyes, the lust of the flesh, and the pride of life. The world system is a system that is built on selfishness, which is why the devil is in control of it. It is predicated on appetites, desires, and mind-sets that contradict what the kingdom of God stands for. Everything in the world system is broken and doomed to fail, which is why Believers must completely disconnect from it. We can't rely on the world for our financial security or our source of health care. Nor can we look to the world system concerning marriage, parenting, or relationships. Everything this world system has to offer is based on lust and pride.

It is so easy to become caught up in the norms and values of society, which are governed by the world. There are so many ideas about what is right and wrong swirling around us every day. Images and words are constantly pumped through the media that are designed to get our focus off the Word of God and on what the world says is acceptable. If we are not vigilant about guarding our hearts and renewing our minds, the subtle deception and seduction of worldly thinking can creep into our consciousness and begin affecting how we think and how we behave. The Bible says that we are in the world but not of it, which means that while we live on this earth, we are going to be surrounded by the corrupt influences of this system of thought that opposes God. However, as Believers, we are called to be the light in the midst of a dark world. Jesus has equipped us with every tool we need to be victorious in this life.

There are so many ideas about what is right and wrong swirling around us every day.

The passage in 1 John 2 is all about allegiance. Allegiance is defined as *loyalty owed to a sovereign nation or cause; fidelity.* When we talk about the world system, which is governed by the law of sin and death, versus the kingdom of God system, which is governed by the law of the spirit of life in Christ Jesus, the issue ultimately boils down to allegiance. The Apostle John is challenging Believers to identify whom they are loyal to. He says that if you love the world, the love of the Father is not in you. It's time to do some self-evaluation. It's time to ask yourself the hard question, *Whom am I loyal to?* Has the world and its way of thinking and doing things become more attractive to you than God's way of doing things? Do you love the things of the world? Have you been seduced into thinking that what God has to offer you is somehow not as appealing or fulfilling as what the world is pushing as desirable? If so, it is time to do a heart check and make some adjustments.

> *It's time to ask yourself the hard question,*
> **Whom am I loyal to?**

The truth is we cannot be in allegiance to the world and God at the same time. We cannot serve two masters. We must make a decision that we are going to choose God's way of doing things no matter what. And why wouldn't we want to? The things of the world, its lusts and pride, are passing away and will eventually come to nothing. To choose the world system as the standard by which you conduct your life is to ultimately choose destruction. God has a better way.

Loyalty to God's Word is what separates those who wear the title of Christian from those who actually follow Christ. Keep in mind that everything in the world is designed to move you into a place of fear, self-preservation, lust, and pride. The enemy works through suggestion in order to get you to take his bait and accept a lie. His ultimate goal is to destroy your life by getting you to come into agreement with his way of doing things (the world's way). On the other hand, God's system of operation is fail-proof and designed to move you into a place of abundance. We have to make a decision of quality to keep our eyes focused on the kingdom of God and not the world.

Loyalty to God's Word is what separates those who wear the title of Christian from those who actually follow Christ.

What Is "the Flesh"?

The issue of "the flesh" is often not clarified in many Christian circles. The term is typically thrown around, but it is not always explained, which can lead to some confusion about it. The flesh is not simply referring to your physical flesh, although your body is composed of literal flesh. When the Bible talks about the "flesh" it is actually talking about a way of thinking that goes against the Word of God.

The flesh is your unrenewed mind, with all its carnal thoughts and desires, along with the residue that was left on your soul from your unsaved state.

In order to better understand the flesh,
it is important to understand the tri-part
nature of man.

In order to better understand the flesh, it is important to understand the tri-part nature of man. As I stated earlier, man is a spirit, who possesses a soul, and lives in a physical body. The soul is made up of the mind, will, and emotions. When you became born again, your spirit was re-created in righteousness and true holiness. The Holy Spirit sealed your spirit, and it is eternally one with God. However, your soul was not born again. This is the area where the "flesh" resides. Like your physical body, it was not made new at the point of salvation. While your spirit looks just like Jesus, your soul is in need of constant renewal, and this is only accomplished through the renewing of the mind with the Word of God (Romans 12:1, 2).

Many times Christians wonder how they could think certain thoughts or participate in certain actions as saved people. The answer is simple. Their spirits are born again, but their minds, wills, and emotions have not been renewed. An unrenewed mind is controlled by the dictates and impulses of the flesh. There are people who accepted Christ but never entered into the mind renewal process as an act of their will. As a result, they deal with the same issues they had when they were unsaved. The only way to see a change in the kind of manifestation you get in your life is to change your thinking, and this only takes place by allowing the Word of God to change your mind-set. You have to meditate on the Word in order to receive God's thoughts.

You have to meditate on the Word in order to receive God's thoughts.

Galatians 5:16–21 describes the works of the flesh and how to avoid participating in them. The formula laid out in the Word is the answer to overriding every flesh-based thought, desire, behavior, and mind-set that the enemy tries to get us to become subject to as Christians. The Apostle Paul was speaking to Believers in this passage, so we know that he was addressing Christians who were dealing with these issues. You are not alone. No one is exempt from being tempted by the suggestions of the devil to succumb to the desires of the unrenewed mind.

Galatians 5:19–21 lists the "works of the flesh" as adultery, fornication, uncleanness, lasciviousness, idolatry, witchcraft, hatred, variance, emulations, wrath, strife, seditions, heresies, envying, murders, drunkenness, revelings, and anything that falls under the umbrella of any of these things. If you, as a Christian, find yourself struggling with any of these things, or falling prey to the enemy's temptations in these areas, understand that your born-again spirit does not participate in the works of the flesh. You engage in these behaviors because you are following the dictates of your carnal mind, rather than your born-again spirit.

Galatians 5:16 tells us how to get out of flesh-led behavior: "This I say then, Walk in the Spirit, and ye shall not fulfil the lust of the flesh." To walk in the Spirit is to walk according to the Word of God. To walk in the flesh is to walk according to the desires of your carnal mind. We walk in the Spirit by allowing the Word of God to govern our thinking and ultimately our behavior. We choose, as an act of our will, to align our thoughts with the Scriptures. Every time we do this, we will find ourselves walking in the Spirit.

We walk in the Spirit by allowing the Word of God to govern our thinking and ultimately our behavior.

One of the things that is important when making adjustments in behavior is to remember the eight steps to your destiny. Everything begins with words that you receive, which in turn shape your thoughts. Thoughts lead to emotions that lead to decisions, and decisions lead to actions. Actions, when performed repeatedly, form habits, which shape your character, and character ultimately takes you to your final destination in life. Since we are dealing with overcoming the "works" of the flesh, we can conclude that we have to stop this process before it gets to the action phase, or acting out phase, which means we have to look at the steps leading up to taking action. This would include words, thoughts, feelings, and decisions.

Every flesh-based action stems first from words that you have received. These words may come from the devil as suggestions to your mind, or even from other people around you. Words can enter your soul through music, television, reading material, and so on. If you find yourself engaging in the works of the flesh, go back to where everything started—words. Recognize that the words you receive will begin to form pictures in your mind, which the enemy will use to create strongholds of thoughts. These thoughts will begin to influence how you feel, and when you are being led by your emotions, you will always make decisions outside the will of God.

The Bible clearly tells us how to deal with thoughts that go against God's Word.

The Bible clearly tells us how to deal with thoughts that go against God's Word in 2 Corinthians 10:4, 5. It says, "For the weapons of our warfare are not carnal, but mighty through God to the pulling down of strongholds; Casting down imaginations, and every high thing that exalteth itself against the knowledge of God, and bringing into captivity every thought to the obedience of Christ." First we see that we don't fight fleshly thoughts and desires with natural weapons. Willpower is even based in self-effort. The only antidote for dealing with the thoughts of the unrenewed mind is the Word of God. When the devil makes suggestions to you in the form of words, or you find yourself thinking about things that don't agree with the Word, you must capture those thoughts and cast them down by declaring the Word of God. Second Corinthians 10:4, 5 is a great passage to declare the moment the flesh tries to rise up and get you to receive ungodly thoughts. Say what the Word of God says and capture thoughts when they come to your mind.

Being conscious of what is going on in your soul is critical to not making the wrong decisions.

Being conscious of what is going on in your soul is critical to not making the wrong decisions. I have found that when people are emotional, they will walk in the flesh. You have to be honest with yourself and be aware of what you are thinking and feeling every moment of the day. If you struggle with sexual lust, for example, and are tempted to act on that lust in some way, take inventory of how you are feeling at the time. Are you sad, depressed, angry, lonely, or frustrated? The flesh can be a temporary outlet that people use to escape some sort of pain or negative emotion they are experiencing. Walking in the Spirit means using the Word of God to fill your voids and correct your emotions, rather than allowing the flesh to give you a temporary "fix" that will only backfire on you later on. When you locate the negative emotion that has the potential to guide you down the path of the flesh, immediately check yourself and consult with the Word. Find out what the Word has to say about what you are feeling. The

Word of God has the answer to *every* negative feeling that you will experience. Instead of just acting on what your flesh is saying, tap into the grace of God! Speak the Word of God and release your faith for Jesus to fulfill whatever need you are looking for in some fleshly behavior. The Holy Spirit is faithful to intervene in those moments of pressure.

Instead of just acting on what your flesh is saying, tap into the grace of God!

We also have to think about the outcome of our choices before we act on them. In addition to locating your emotional state before making certain decisions, take a moment to play out the end result of making that flesh-led decision in your mind. One thing is for sure, no matter how good something looks or how enticing it appears, if it is a suggestion of the devil, or a work of the flesh, it is *always* going to lead to some sort of destruction and *never* has any profit attached to it. It will never benefit your spiritual life or edify you. All it will do is break your soul down and invite negative consequences into your life. Galatians 6:7, 8 says, "Be not deceived; God is not mocked: for whatsoever a man soweth, that shall he also reap. For he that soweth to his flesh shall of the flesh reap corruption; but he that soweth to the Spirit shall of the Spirit reap life everlasting."

The flesh is designed to lead you into a place of sin and ultimately bring corruption into your life. I don't care how harmless it may seem. Anything that can be classified as a work of the flesh is detrimental to your life. You can begin to improve the quality of your life by making choices in line with the Word (walking in the Spirit) and turning away from those things that are detrimental to your spiritual well-being. Be honest with yourself and stop the process of flesh-led living by being a custodian over your thought life and allowing your emotions to be subject to the Word of God. The flesh has no profit.

You can begin to improve the quality of your life by making choices in line with the Word.

Satan: The "God" of This World

The unholy trinity would not be complete without addressing the devil. Contrary to what the majority of people in the world think, the devil does indeed exist. He has many names in the Bible, but the one that I want to focus on is "adversary." He is referred to as the "god of this world," meaning he is the god/ruler of this present world system in which we live. Remember, the "world" refers to the mind-sets, systems, institutions, and ways of doing things that go against the Word of God. These are the arenas over which Satan presides and through which he operates on this earth. He is not a fictional character or figment of the imagination. He is an actual spiritual being whose one and only goal is to destroy you.

As a Christian, you have an adversary, or enemy, and he is constantly seeking whom he can devour.

First Peter 5:8 says, "Be sober, be vigilant; because your adversary the devil, as a roaring lion, walketh about, seeking whom he may devour." As a Christian, you have an adversary, or enemy, and he is constantly seeking whom he can devour. The fact that he is looking for those who can be devoured lets us know that not everyone is "devourable." He searches for those who are more loyal to the world's way of doing things than they are to God. He looks for people who allow their flesh to rule their lives, rather than the Word of God. He is aware of your weaknesses, and he will try to use them against you. Second Thessalonians 2:10 says that he uses unlimited seduction and all kinds of wicked deception to lead people astray. He doesn't play fair. In order to avoid being devoured, it is critical that you make the Word of God your final authority and make walking in the Spirit your priority as a Believer.

You may think that you have no power over the enemy's suggestions and temptations. You may have fallen into sin so many times that you've given up hope of ever coming out of the behavior or mind-set you're involved with. Don't believe Satan's lies and attempts to make you feel condemned and hopeless.

Don't believe Satan's lies and attempts to make you feel condemned and hopeless.

As a Believer, you have been empowered with the grace of God to live a life that pleases God—a life that is not governed by the flesh, the world, and the devil. Titus 2:11, 12 gives us an encouraging word on the grace of God and how it enables us to live godly lives: "For the grace of God that bringeth salvation hath appeared to all men, Teaching us that, denying ungodliness and worldly lusts, we should live soberly, righteously, and godly, in this present world." Wow! The grace of God is a supernatural empowerment from God that enables us to carry out God's instructions to us. He would never tell us to do something that He didn't equip us to do. Our "equipment" is the grace of God, which resides in us through Jesus Christ. When we release our faith in this grace, we find the spiritual fortitude to turn away from, or "deny" as the scripture says, ungodliness and worldly lusts. This grace empowers us to live "soberly," righteously, and godly in the midst of an evil world. To live a sober life is essentially to live a life in which your thinking is not intoxicated by the world's ideas and ways of doing things. The sober life is the life that Satan cannot overpower.

Our "equipment" is the grace of God, which resides in us through Jesus Christ.

James 4:7 gives a clear directive on how to get the devil out of your life. It says we are to submit to God and resist the devil. Submission is a heart attitude and a decision that takes place before you even outwardly do anything. A heart that is submitted to God is committed to obeying the Word in all situations and circumstances. In the position of submission, there is an empowerment and there is protection from God. When the devil sees that you are submitted to the Word of God, committed and loyal to God's way of doing things, and that you are resisting his suggestions by casting down thoughts, speaking God's Word, and making decisions that are aligned with God's will for your life, *he will flee.* You don't have to try to get him to flee when the Bible gives a clear formula to follow: submit and resist. It is in your submission and resistance to Satan that you force him to retreat.

No one said being a Christian would be easy.

No one said being a Christian would be easy. Every day that we wake up, we are in an all-out battle against an enemy who constantly uses strategies and plans to destroy our lives. However, Jesus has already given us the victory! If you are in Christ, you are seated with Him in heavenly places, which means you are operating from a position of spiritual authority over Satan. By following God's instructions to walk in the Spirit, cast down imaginations, submit to His Word, and resist the suggestions of the enemy, you can gain mastery over any habit, behavior, or temptation in your life. You have the Word of God, the blood of Jesus, the Holy Spirit, and the grace of God available to you. Your victory over the world, the flesh, and the devil has already been secured. All you have to do is walk in it by faith.

8

FOUR AREAS OF STRUGGLE

Wherewithal shall a young man cleanse
his way? by taking heed thereto according
to thy word.
With my whole heart have I sought thee:
O let me not wander from thy
commandments.
Thy word have I hid in mine heart,
that I might not sin against thee.

—PSALM 119:9–11

In all things shewing thyself a pattern of good
works: in doctrine shewing uncorruptness,
gravity, sincerity...

—TITUS 2:7

Being a man in today's world is not easy. There are so many opportunities for us to stray from God's way of doing things and embrace the world's way of thinking. The enemy is constantly looking for inroads into our lives by trying to influence our thinking to go in a direction that disagrees with the Word. I have discovered that there are four areas in which Satan typically attacks men, and it is not a coincidence. God made us to be a particular way for a particular reason. We are providers, and we thrive when we achieve great things. We are created to be the spiritual heads of our households, and to lead others as we follow Christ's example. It is no surprise, then, that the four main areas of struggle for men deal with our spiritual lives with God, finances, lust, and achievement. When we understand these areas and how to keep them submitted to the Word of God, we can be most effective as men of God.

Every man has his own battle—that one thing that he may deal with on a personal basis.

Every man has his own battle—that one thing that he may deal with on a personal basis. Not every person has the same struggle, but Satan is unrelenting in his assaults on the minds and hearts of men. That has always been his plan, because he hates mankind. Men (and women) are created in the image of God, and Satan hates God. So naturally, when he sees us, he sees a reflection of God, something he will never have the opportunity to experience. He is forever locked out of communion and fellowship with the Father, and he desires us to be separated from Him as well. Fortunately, when you are born again, you have an advocate with the Father—Jesus Christ—and nothing can separate you from His love for you. This simply means that no matter what you are going through, or may be struggling with, God's love and grace are constantly available to you.

First Things First

Our relationship with God is the most important thing in our lives, and if it isn't a priority, it must become our priority. This is the foundation for our success and victory, which is why husbands, fathers, brothers, sons, whether single or married, must make spending time with God our highest order of the day. Cultivating an ongoing relationship with the Lord is essential to maintaining close communion and fellowship with Him. This is the primary area the enemy will attack. Let's look at some foundational aspects of developing our spiritual life that are critical to our growth and development:

1. Prayer

Prayer is absolutely vital to our spiritual lives because it plugs us into the power of God. When we pray, we are communicating with God and allowing Him to speak to us. I look at prayer as a dialogue, not a monologue, meaning we are not the only ones doing the talking. When we pray, we should take time to talk to God and give Him a chance to respond. It is in the place of prayer that we receive instruction, direction, correction, and insight for our daily lives.

When we pray, we are communicating with God and allowing Him to speak to us.

As men, it is important that we spend time praying, and we should pray in different ways. God has given us His Word as well as a heavenly prayer language that allows us to directly communicate to

God, spirit to Spirit, without interference from the devil. Praying in tongues is one of the most effective ways we can pray the will of God as well as build ourselves up in faith and love. Every Christian man needs to use this powerful prayer tool on a frequent basis.

The Apostle Paul gives a clear directive about prayer in Ephesians 6:18: "Praying always with all prayer and supplication in the Spirit, and watching thereunto with all perseverance and supplications for all saints." Paul is admonishing Believers to put on the whole armor of God in the previous verses, and he finishes up with the weapon of prayer. He says we are to *always* pray *in the Spirit* with all kinds of prayers. He also tells us we must persevere in prayer and pray for other Christians as well. Paul was a man of prayer who spent time praying in the Spirit frequently. Looking at his ministry and the results he received makes it clear why prayer is so important.

---

*Jesus is our best example to follow
as it relates to prayer.*

Jesus is our best example to follow as it relates to prayer. He was God in the flesh, yet the Bible says that He would get up early to pray and commune with the Father. Matthew 14:23 says, "And when he had sent the multitudes away, he went up into a mountain apart to pray: and when the evening was come, he was there alone." Mark 1:35 describes Jesus' early morning prayer habit when it says, "And in the morning, rising up a great while before day, he went out, and departed into a solitary place, and there prayed." Luke 5:16 says that Jesus withdrew to deserted places to pray, particularly after ministering to large crowds of people. The place of prayer was a place of spiritual rejuvenation for the Lord, where He was able to recharge His spiritual batteries. We should follow His example.

Jesus' spiritual life and communion with the Father through prayer were also the source of His power. He only did and said what the Father told Him to do and say (John 12:49; John 5:30; John 8:28; John 5:19). Imagine how much more effective we would be in our relationships, marriages, jobs, and ministries if we would follow in Jesus' footsteps and make prayer and fellowship with the Father our highest priority. He got results *every* time because He was able to hear exactly what to do in every situation. This is the key to our success, and it only comes by developing the spiritual disciplines necessary to get supernatural results.

2. The Word of God

Spending time in the Word every day is the other life essential if we want our spiritual lives to be well-developed. Just as food provides our bodies with nourishment and strength to perform our daily tasks, the Word of God is the spiritual food that sustains our spirits, anchors our souls, and provides us with the strength we need to withstand the attacks of the enemy. If you don't feed on the Word, you will become an easy target for Satan to deceive you and get you off track. Your attitude, words, and responses to life will be out of whack when you haven't been spending time in the Word of God. You will have a tendency to go in the direction of your flesh, rather than your spirit, when this area of your life is deficient.

Spending time in the Word every day is the other life essential if we want our spiritual lives to be well-developed.

I can always tell when someone hasn't been spending time in the Word. Think about when you don't eat for long periods of time. You are tired, cranky, and often can't think clearly. This is because your body is deficient of the nutrients it needs. You wouldn't go an entire week without eating any food or drinking any water. If you did, your body would begin to shut down. So likewise, we should never go a day without "eating" the living bread of God's Word. Not only do we need to eat the Word on a daily basis, but we must meditate on it as well. This would be the equivalent of chewing natural food. Joshua 1:8 says that when we meditate on the Word day and night, our way becomes prosperous and we have good success. When we meditate on the Word, we are chewing it and digesting it so that it can go deep into our hearts and ultimately change the way we think. This is another discipline that is absolutely critical to our spiritual lives.

We should never go a day without "eating"
the living bread of God's Word.

Everything starts with our spiritual lives. If we want to see changes in our lives, our foundations must be intact. The Word, prayer, and intimate fellowship with God on a daily basis are what keep us going strong.

Finances: Prospering God's Way

Another area in which men struggle is finances. This is an area that is directly tied to our sense of accomplishment, success, and the ability to provide. When a man is not making the kind of money he wants to make, he can become extremely frustrated, especially if he has a wife and/or children. The enemy will attack a man's sense of worth when he doesn't have much in his bank account, particularly in a society that is driven by image and materialism. As men, we have to seek God where our finances are concerned and tap into the kingdom of God system in order to meet our needs and the needs of our families.

The enemy will attack a man's sense of worth when he doesn't have much in his bank account, particularly in a society that is driven by image and materialism.

It is difficult to avoid the constant pressure to prosper according to the world's standards. Many men find themselves caught up in a cycle of trying to keep up with the Joneses in an attempt to appear prosperous, when, in reality, their financial situation is the exact opposite. Having the latest gadgets, cars, clothes, and a certain income turns into an elusive dream that men chase, yet, as Christians, there is a way to prosper in God's kingdom that is far superior to the world's way. In God's system, there is no need for competition because there is more than enough for everyone. God wants to prosper you financially, but it's going to take commitment to do things His way.

Matthew 6:33 is the foundation scripture we should be standing on as it relates to our finances. You may be familiar with it: "But seek ye first the kingdom of God, and his righteousness; and all these things shall be added unto you." What is the kingdom of God? It is God's way of doing things. God's way of doing things involves a simple process called seedtime and harvest. This is the process by which *everything* we obtain from God comes into our lives.

God's way of doing things involves a simple process called seedtime and harvest.

It is indeed God's will to prosper us in our finances, but it's important to keep finances in their proper perspective. God never intended for money to rule our lives, or the desire to obtain it to consume us. We must rest in the fact that God is our Provider and He will provide all our needs (Philippians 4:19). So what should be our attitude regarding finances, and how can we guard against the attacks of the enemy in this area?

First, we must recognize that God is our source. Not only that, but He is our *only* source. We can never rely on self-effort or other people as an acceptable means of getting our needs met. God has many channels and avenues through which His resources can flow into our lives, but He is the ultimate source of our provision. We must remember that our jobs are not our source, but rather they are assignments we are to embrace as part of our service to the Lord. When we are faithful to the assignments God has given us, we will reap the benefits of our faithfulness. But we can never get to the place where we start trusting the avenue for the provision more than we do the real source—God.

We can never rely on self-effort or other people as an acceptable means of getting our needs met.

The second important key to this area of financial increase is recognizing that we must engage the process of seedtime and harvest in order to see results in our finances. Genesis 8:22 says that as long as the earth remains, seedtime and harvest will not cease. Seedtime and harvest is the process whereby we get our needs met by God. It is the process that involves our planting a seed and getting a return on the seed we plant. Second Corinthians chapter 9 gives some wonderful insight into the mentality God wants us to have as it relates to sowing, or giving. Verse 6 says, "He which soweth sparingly shall reap also sparingly; and he which soweth bountifully shall reap also bountifully." In essence, God is saying that the level of your giving determines the type of harvest you receive. The more you give, the more you can expect to receive.

The more you give, the more you can expect to receive.

If you are releasing your faith for a bigger financial harvest, take a look at the type of seeds you have been sowing. Verse 7 says that God loves a cheerful giver and verse 8 of that same chapter says that God will cause all grace to abound toward you so that you will always have enough to meet every need and obligation. These are promises from God! Embracing God's way of doing things is a fail-proof method to prosper financially.

Jesus tells us that we should not be troubled by the things we see going on in this world. Financial and economic challenges are everywhere we turn, and the world is feeling the brunt of a failing financial system that is only going to continue to deteriorate. But there is good news for you! If you are in the family of God, you are not bound by the economic downturns that the world experiences, neither do you have to worry about your financial well-being. God will do more than what you could imagine when you simply release your faith in His Word. Not only can He take care of you financially, but He *will*. God will not only bring money into your hands to cover your own needs, but He will also bless you with more than enough so that you can help others as well. This is true prosperity.

God will do more than what you could imagine when you simply release your faith in His Word.

The third key to keep in mind regarding finances is that as men, we have to always remember that our worth and identity are *not* found in how much is in our bank accounts. I say this because there are many men who struggle with feelings of inadequacy when they compare themselves to other men who may have more in their bank accounts. This is dangerous thinking because it opens the door to envy, jealousy, and insecurity, three emotions that the enemy will capitalize on if we are not careful.

Who you are in Christ is what shapes your identity, not your bank account balance.

Who you are in Christ is what shapes your identity, not your bank account balance. You may have been raised in a family that put a high premium on making six figures, or you may be surrounded with other men who have more than you may have at the moment. Or you may be a man who has achieved a level of financial success and have lost sight of the fact that your money does not define you as a man. No matter what your salary is, your sense of identity must be firmly grounded in the fact that you are a son of God and you hold unlimited potential because of *who* lives in you, not how much you make. You possess the source of prosperity within your born-again spirit, and when you possess the source, the outward manifestation of that prosperity will come as you learn to walk according to the Word of God and activate the spiritual principles outlined in the Bible. Never allow comparisons or bank account balances to rob you of your true identity in Christ. You are loved by God and empowered by grace to succeed in the financial arena.

Lust: Battling Unhealthy Desires

The area of lust is one that every man has dealt with in his life in some form or another. Sexual lust, in particular, is probably the most universal struggle that men go through. Some are more proficient at keeping their flesh in check than others, but the temptation to lust is everywhere we turn. We must make a conscious decision to choose purity rather than giving in to our flesh. It is a decision we have to make every day of our lives. Don't ever fall for the lie, "I just can't help it." The grace of God has empowered Believers with the ability to please Him through our thoughts, words, and actions.

Don't ever fall for the lie, "I just can't help it."

Our society and popular culture are saturated with images, words, pictures, and outlets that are designed to feed lustful appetites into men and women. It's the billboard of the half-naked woman looming above the freeway as you drive home from work, the explicit sex scene that flashes before your eyes in the movie theater, the pornographic sites that are accessible through your computer or cell phone, and the suggestive song lyrics and videos that are pumped through the media. It is the whisper of the enemy to look a second and third time at an attractive woman standing in the checkout line at the grocery store. We live in this world, but the Bible says we are not of this world. However, God will not force us to keep lust out of our hearts. It is up to us to implement self-discipline as it relates to what we allow into our hearts, and we must release our faith in the grace of God, which empowers us to please Him in our thoughts, words, and deeds.

Lust is simply a desire that is outside the will of God.

Lust is simply a desire that is outside the will of God. God gave us the desire for food, for example, but when we allow our appetite for food to control our lives and inform our choices to the point where we are engaging in destructive behavior, we are operating in gluttony, which stems from lust. Sexual desire in and of itself is normal and healthy; it is a God-given desire that is a part of the human experience. However, it turns into lust when we start desiring things that are outside the will of God for our lives.

When people allow lust to take up residence in their hearts, they start a process of desiring things that are not in line with God's Word, and they also turn on appetites that can never be satisfied. That is in essence the nature of lust: a desire that can never be satisfied. The man who indulges in pornography can never get enough pornography, even though he tells himself that this will be the last time he watches it. The act of fornication is essentially unsatisfying because the person who engages in it can never get enough. He will seek an orgasm with whomever he can, whenever he can, even at the expense of another person or his own well-being; however, he will still walk away empty and unfulfilled. That's the thing about lust; it never comes to the end of itself. Like a fire that requires more wood in order to burn, lust continually requires that you feed it. It never says, *enough*.

Men are visual, which is why it is no surprise that Satan continually seeks to assault our eyes with images that are designed to turn on lustful desires.

His objective is to steal, kill, and destroy our lives by getting us trapped in unhealthy behavior that consumes us. In order to avoid falling victim to lust traps, we must be vigilant about what we allow to come through our eyes, go into our ears, and come out of our mouths, because these are the things that will ultimately shape our lives (Proverbs 4:23). *We have to monitor the things we look at, listen to, and talk about*, because if we let lustful, sexually charged imagery into our hearts, we will find ourselves being controlled by desires that are not within the parameters of God's Word. God will not do this for us; it is up to us to make the decision to turn away from things that ignite the flames of lust.

**We *have to monitor the things we look at,
listen to, and talk about.***

Job 31:1 gives us a good starting point for guarding our eyes since, for men, the eye gate is one of the most vulnerable targets of the enemy. It says, *"I made a covenant with my eyes not to look lustfully at a girl."* Job had made a decision to make an agreement with his own eyes and not allow himself to look at a woman with lust in his heart. That's a pretty bold commitment! I think this would be a good time to clarify the difference between admiring a beautiful woman and lusting after her. Let's face it, women are beautiful creations! There is nothing wrong with acknowledging to yourself that a woman is pretty or attractive. Lust begins to enter the picture when you start desiring that woman in a sexual way or fantasizing about her. Whether you are married or single, desiring or fantasizing about a woman who is not your wife is not the will of God. Will the enemy tempt you in this area? Yes! But those are the times when you must cast down ungodly imaginations by capturing the thoughts with the Word of God. Those are the times when you have to bounce your eyes away and train yourself in this area. When you find yourself tempted to lust after someone, open your mouth and declare what the Word of God says. Command your thoughts to line up with the Word. They have no choice but to submit to that authority.

There is nothing wrong with acknowledging to yourself that a woman is pretty or attractive.

We also have to renew our minds to what the word of God says about this issue. Many men were raised with the false idea that there is nothing wrong with looking lustfully at a woman or engaging in pornography. Some men were even told that there was something wrong with them if they *didn't* engage in these behaviors.

Parents, family members, and friends shape the way we think about sex, sexuality, and what is appropriate behavior for men. In a culture and society that celebrate men who can get as many women in bed as possible, it can be a task to break the strongholds that many of us have grown up believing are acceptable male behavior. As Christians, we must acquire a new mind-set by allowing the Word to wash all of that junk out of our minds, and also by seeing women the way God sees them: as valuable, precious, and made in His image. When we lust after women in a sexual way, we essentially devalue them by turning them into sexual objects. This is not the way God wants us to think. He holds us to a higher standard than the worldly guy who doesn't know any better, because He has given us His grace, His Word, the Holy Spirit, and the blood of Jesus. We have all the tools we need to be men of integrity, honor, and purity in every aspect of our lives.

Parents, family members, and friends shape the way we think about sex, sexuality, and what is appropriate behavior for men.

Choosing to walk in sexual purity is a decision that starts long before a temptation shows up. It starts with a commitment to God to honor His Word and His way of doing things. Meditate on the Word and begin to renew your mind to the way God sees you and others. Exercise self-discipline where your eyes are concerned by practicing bouncing your eyes away from the image or person that has the potential to become a temptation. Don't actively seek out environments, people, and images that fan the flames of lust. Choose to honor God, and He will honor you.

Meditate on the Word and begin to renew your mind to the way God sees you and others.

Be a Receiver, Not an "Achiever"

The fourth area that tends to be a challenge for men is the area of achievement. Men are achievement-driven, and we tend to derive our sense of purpose and worth from the things we achieve, whether professionally, financially, or even in our relationships. Unfortunately, we can get so wrapped up in achievement and acquiring a certain level of success that we can lose sight of our relationship with God. Not only that, but it is very easy for men to get into a cycle of trying to make things happen themselves, which is essentially self-effort. The moment we start trusting in ourselves rather than God, we begin to lose our way. God wants us to be less focused on achieving and more focused on receiving from Him. After all, He is our only source.

Understanding God's grace is critical to being able to transition from an achieving mentality to a receiving mentality. Grace has made available to us everything we will ever need in this life. Our success and prosperity are found in Christ, and we access these things through the empowerment, or ability, we possess through Him. We received our salvation by grace, through faith, and this salvation includes not only our eternal destination but our deliverance, healing, wholeness, and prosperity. When we have confidence in what God has invested in us, we are able to pursue His will for our lives without fear. Our futures are secure when we receive what God has done for us.

Grace has made available to us everything
we will ever need in this life.

One of the keys to being a receiver is having a revelation that everything we try to obtain in this life originates in the spiritual realm. You are not trying to make something happen; you are acknowledging that God has *already* made His blessings available to you. All you have to do is receive them by faith and position yourself to walk in them. Stop trying to come up with your own plan about how you are going to get things to work and start trusting in God. The spiritual realm is the parent realm of your financial prosperity, the career God has for you, a successful marriage, and everything else promised in His Word that pertains to life and godliness.

Ephesians 1:3 says, "Blessed be the God and Father of our Lord Jesus Christ, who hath blessed us with all spiritual blessings in the heavenly places in Christ." You possess the spiritual blessings that are necessary to be the man God has called you to be and to achieve all that He has called you to achieve. Ultimately, the achievement you are after is fulfilling the will of God for your life. It's not about pursuing the path that you've carved out for yourself but about walking out the path that God has prepared for you before the foundations of the world. On His path is the abundance, fulfillment, and peace that you are looking for.

*You possess the spiritual blessings that are
necessary to be the man God has called you to
be and to achieve all that He has called you
to achieve.*

If you want to be one of those men whom God calls "good" and "faithful," then hearing His voice is critical. Jesus had success and achieved tangible results everywhere He went because He heard and obeyed the voice of His Father. Achievement in the kingdom of God is based on your hearing God's instructions and doing whatever He tells *you* to do. When you receive a word from the Lord, you don't have to try to do anything in your own ability. You simply follow His instructions, which always lead to success. It's not about how many degrees you have or what your credentials are. Putting your trust in God and standing on His Word with unwavering commitment are what position you for success. There is no fear in God, who is love. Your confidence in His love and ability is what gives you the edge in life.

*Your confidence in His love and ability is
what gives you the edge in life.*

Philemon 1:6 tells us to acknowledge those good things God has placed within us. Confess that you possess success on the inside of you because Jesus lives in you. Boldly declare that you are equipped with the grace to do everything God has called you to do. Most important, *receive* the finished work of Christ in your life. Meditate on the Word of God until it becomes more real to you than anything else. As the Word begins to anchor your soul, you will be able to walk in the grace of God for kingdom achievement, knowing that whether it is dealing with your walk with God, your finances, living a life of purity, or personal achievement, it is not your own effort that will get the job done, but God working in and through your life. He is the author and the finisher of your faith, and He is bringing to completion the work He started in you.

9

FANTASY: ADDICTED TO THE COUNTERFEIT

Husbands, love your wives, even as Christ also loved the church, and gave himself for it . . .

—EPHESIANS 5:25

Likewise, ye husbands, dwell with [them] according to knowledge, giving honour unto the wife, as unto the weaker vessel, and as being heirs together of the grace of life; that your prayers be not hindered.

—1 PETER 3:7

So God created man in His *own* image; in the image of God He created him; male and female He created them.

—GENESIS 1:27

It's no secret that pornography is a huge part of today's society. The objectification of women and girls is everywhere, and it is constantly shaping how men and women see each other and themselves. Not only that, but pornography is a multibillion-dollar industry that thrives on the weaknesses of the flesh. So many men find themselves caught in the throes of pornography addiction and have no idea how to get out or how to turn off the desire for porn that they have ignited. Like any addictive behavior, addiction to porn begins when you allow sexually explicit material into your heart through your eye gate, which in turn begins the process of forming strongholds in your mind that become difficult to dismantle. Pornography essentially sells a lie, and that lie is that you can actually achieve sexual and emotional satisfaction by indulging in pornographic material. It is an attempt to achieve intimacy and fill a void through a counterfeit method. The problem is that lust can never be satisfied, and neither can the desire for pornography. Only when you get a revelation of God's love for you and His desire to fulfill all of your deepest needs can you begin the process of deliverance from this deadly spiritual poison.

I have actually heard men say that watching pornography is a normal activity for a healthy male. Men who do not indulge in pornographic material are often looked at as abnormal by the carnally minded man. It seems almost unfathomable to some men that there are those who don't engage in sexually reckless behavior that objectifies women in some form or another. The idea is that healthy male sexuality is based on how lustful and insatiable your sexual appetite is. If you don't fit this mold, something is wrong with you.

The truth is that every man and woman was created in God's image, to fulfill His purpose of glorifying Him with every aspect of who they are.

These ideas about men's sexuality are so far from the truth of God's Word and how God created men that it is embarrassing. The devil has sold us this lie for too long, and it is time to uncover the truth. The truth is that every man and woman was created in God's image, to fulfill His purpose of glorifying Him with every aspect of who they are. Pornography is a direct assault on the image of humanity and a cheapening of the beautiful gift of sexuality that God has imparted into every human being. By turning sex into a product, pornography takes away from the humanity of people and brings them to the lowest possible level. Repeatedly indulging in adult "entertainment" will eventually shape how you see yourself and others, whether you realize it or not.

Before we get into the real meat of this issue, I want to take a moment to share the eight-step progression to a person's destiny. The progression begins with words, which shape your thoughts. Your thoughts will give birth to emotions, and emotions will lead you to make certain decisions. Decisions lead to actions, which lead to habits, which ultimately shape your character. And your character is what is going to move you to your final destination, or destiny in life.

Decisions lead to actions, which lead to habits, which ultimately shape your character.

There is no escaping this "chain of destiny" because it is based on spiritual laws that are constantly in operation. Spiritual laws don't discriminate; they will work for anyone who will get involved with them (knowingly or unknowingly). The law of seedtime and harvest is the primary law in operation in this process. Whatever you plant in your heart through what you look at, listen to, and talk about is a seed that *will* produce a harvest one day. Galatians 6:7 says, "Be not deceived; God is not mocked: for whatsoever a man soweth, that shall he also reap." The Word of God is crystal clear. Whatever you sow, you will reap. Verse 8 says, "For he that soweth to his flesh shall of the flesh reap corruption; but he that soweth to the Spirit shall of the Spirit reap life everlasting." We have to constantly remind ourselves that the flesh has *no profit*. That means that the inevitable outcome of any flesh-led or carnally minded decision is going to be no profit and corruption. There is no way around this spiritual principle of seedtime and harvest.

With that being said, it is essential that we understand how the heart, or spirit, of a man works. Your spirit is the core of who you are, and it can be likened to fertile soil that is waiting for seed to be planted. No one knows how or why a seed is able to do what it does once it is planted in soil, but the process is always the same. Once a seed is planted, the soil and the seed work together to cause that seed to break open, grow roots, and eventually grow into a plant or tree of some sort that will bear some kind of fruit or flower. This is why Proverbs 4:23 instructs us to guard our hearts; the issues of our lives flow out of what is planted there. If your heart is filled with pornography, it is only a matter of time before the issues arising from that addiction begin to affect your life and the lives of those around you. Don't be deceived. What you plant in your heart *will* eventually overtake and overwhelm your life. It's a spiritual law.

Your spirit is the core of who you are, and it can be likened to fertile soil that is waiting for seed to be planted.

Understanding the Lie of Porn

Pornography is a subject that many people are uncomfortable talking about, particularly those who consume it and are addicted to it. Many have accepted it as a normal way of looking at women and sexual relationships, and they don't want to be challenged about it. However, pornography is spiritual poison that contaminates a person's soul and hinders his fellowship with God and others. Like any addiction, it becomes the centerpiece of a person's life— an idol that can be extremely difficult to let go of.

Only through the grace of God and the power of the Holy Spirit can deliverance take place.

Why is pornography so problematic? Well, first and foremost, it is a form of sexual immorality, which is clearly a violation of God's Word. Pornography also dishonors the image of God in an individual by treating him or her as a sexual object to be consumed directly or indirectly.

Pornography also dishonors the image of God in an individual by treating him or her as a sexual object to be consumed directly or indirectly.

Pornography is derived from the Greek word *porne,* which can be translated as "female captives" or "prostitutes." *Porneia* is often translated as "fornication," "whoredom," or "sexual immorality." In the New Testament, there are twenty-six references to *porneia*. Of these twenty-six, six occur in First and Second Corinthians. The context of these writings is that Christians are not to conform to the norms and values of society, which at that time (and today) involved *porneia,* or sexual immorality. The Word clearly tells us that our bodies were not created for *porneia,* and we should run in fear from sexual immorality in all its forms (1 Corinthians 6:18). We shouldn't seek it out (1 Corinthians 7:2), and we should repent of it if we fall prey to it (2 Corinthians 12:21). Pornography literally involves every manner of sexual immorality from homosexuality to bestiality. The pornography industry has capitalized on the commercialization and commodification of human sexuality, just like prostitution. It is no different. When you watch it and use it, you are engaging in a form of prostitution, even if it is done from the comfort of your own home.

Pornography takes the gift of human sexuality out of its proper and natural context—intimacy between two human beings—and makes it a product to be bought and sold. By debasing the human body and valuing it on the same level as an item you would buy at a convenience store, it promotes the idea that human sexuality is nothing more than something to be used and ultimately thrown away. Women and men who work in the sex industry are dispensable and are viewed as "product," not human beings. When you indulge in pornography, you are not only hurting your own soul, but you are supporting an industry that, at its very core, is designed to turn human sexuality into a product.

Whether it is strip clubs, Internet porn, phone sex lines, or videos, pornography preys on two groups of people: the consumer and the individuals being consumed (the sex industry workers). When you peruse pornographic websites, rent porn movies, or buy magazines, you add to the demand for pornography. You may not be doing anything illegal per se, but you are fueling the demand for pornography from the industry that produces it. You are contributing to a problem and helping to keep yourself and those you are viewing on the screen or in the magazine in bondage. We have to start looking at our actions in terms of the bigger picture, and realize that our behavior affects others. Everything we do is a seed that reaps either corruption or godly character in our lives and in the lives of others.

Everything we do is a seed that reaps either corruption or godly character in our lives and in the lives of others.

Pornography use in and of itself is extremely selfish. As I mentioned earlier, it sells a lie that tells people they can achieve satisfaction and fulfillment from indulging in these images. However, the nature of porn is lust, and lust is never satisfied. It is an attempt to achieve intimacy in the deepest parts of our being, intimacy that can only be achieved through our relationship and fellowship with God, which He desires to cultivate with us through prayer and spending time in His Word and His presence. When you continually turn to pornography to gratify a selfish desire, it is an indication that you are spiritually empty and are in desperate need of renewed fellowship with the Father. He loves you and desires to fill you with his joy, grace, and peace.

Pornography: An Assault on Your Soul

I often talk about soul prosperity when I teach about the prosperous life. Prosperity of soul is the key to living the abundant life. Third John 2 says, "Beloved, I wish above all things that mayest prosper and be in health, even as thy soul prospers." The Apostle John was talking about his desire for the readers of his letter to be healthy and whole in their minds, wills, and emotions. This is what true prosperity is all about because it is from a prosperous soul that the other areas of our life prosper and flourish.

*What we allow into our minds is going
to have the effect of feeding us either
nourishment that produces a healthy mind-set
and life, or the exact opposite.*

What we allow into our minds is going to have the effect of feeding us either nourishment that produces a healthy mind-set and life, or the exact opposite. To be poor in soul is to have a mind, will, and emotions that are degenerated, dis-eased, in turmoil and torment, and producing fruit that is inconsistent with the Word of God. The Word of God is food that feeds the spirit and soul. It is living bread, the Bible says, and gives us the spiritual sustenance we need to live healthy, Christ-centered lives. When we read and meditate on the Word of God and fill our minds with material that glorifies God and lines up with the Word, it nourishes us spiritually, mentally, and physically. It can bring healing to the body and wholeness to the soul.

Further, I want to address the soul "poverty" that takes place when you fill your mind with pornographic images. Just as food is consumed and digested by the body, pornography is consumed by the senses and digested by the brain. In the natural digestive process, food is broken down so that it can provide the body with energy that can be used. Waste products and toxins are excreted to ensure that the body stays healthy. If you don't use the bathroom and get rid of waste, you can literally suffer from internal poisoning, and your body will begin to shut down. Similarly, pornographic images are taken into the brain through the senses (the eye gate primarily); however, there is no process through which spiritual "waste" products and residue associated with porn can be removed. Moreover, there is also a physiological response in the brain of a man to pornography that is very similar to what happens when cocaine is ingested. There are even certain physical and neurological changes that actually occur in the brain that contribute to porn's addictive nature. Pornography is, in essence, the consumption of sexual poison that literally becomes part of the fabric of a man's mind. A mind consumed with pornography is a mind that is suffering from soul "poverty."

As Believers we are instructed to think on those things that are honest, pure, just, lovely, and of a good report. We are told to keep our minds stayed on God, and He will keep us in perfect peace. Our whole being, all of our faculties, are to be fully given to God and used for His glory. When we allow our bodily members, including our eyes, to be given over to pornography, we yield to Satan and allow him access into our lives. We are not glorifying God or putting ourselves in a position to receive His best for our lives.

Our whole being, all of our faculties, are to be fully given to God and used for His glory.

Because human sexuality is such an intricate part of us, and it was designed to play a role in the process of developing intimacy, it makes sense that the enemy uses this area to try to provide a counterfeit sense of intimacy. Fulfilling sexual desire is pleasurable because God made it that way. But remember, any time something is used outside of its God-given context and purpose, it becomes perverted or twisted. The appetite for sexual and emotional intimacy through porn is a desire that is outside of God's will because it is turning to something ungodly to fulfill a God-given desire. Through it, a man begins to direct his sexual desires in inappropriate ways that dishonor God, himself, and the individuals he is watching perform the sex acts. It not only becomes a counterfeit method of getting your needs met, but also becomes an idol in your life.

*But remember, any time something is used
outside of its God-given context and purpose,
it becomes perverted or twisted.*

Negative Effects of Pornography on Relationships

Any man who is involved with pornography, whether married or single, positions himself for some very interesting challenges as it relates to his relationships with others, particularly women. Because of the fantasy nature of pornography, it prevents men from being able to see women as they truly are—created in God's image. Women are reduced to sexual objects to be used and discarded, and that mentality will eventually carry over into real-life relationships. It even renders men less sexually responsive to *real* women by numbing a man's healthy sexuality. The need for more and different types of pornography begins to shape a man's thinking to where he can no longer be satisfied with his wife. Single men who are pornography users can begin to have fantasies about being with the images of the types of women viewed in pornography to the point where he begins to seek out these images in real life. Women who don't fit that image become undesirable.

As with any form of "entertainment," it is
important to remember that much of what we
see on our televisions and on the Internet is
not a real representation of life or real people.

As with any form of "entertainment," it is important to remember that much of what we see on our
televisions and on the Internet is not a real representation of life or real people. The strip club dancer
does not really desire the men who patronize her. The
actors and actresses in pornography are not really
enjoying the sexual acts they perform. Pornography
is the farthest from reality when it comes to sexual
relationships. The fantasy quality of it undoubt-
edly contributes to its lure. False intimacy is sought
out without having to engage or interact with an
actual person in a meaningful way. Sexual needs
are attempted to be met without having to invest in
a relationship with a live human being who walks,
talks, and requires attention. Men can become
addicted to the idea of a woman on their computer
or television screen, in a club or in a magazine, fulfilling their sexual desires without any demands for
respect or communication. Unfortunately, when a
man becomes trapped in addictive behavior, he realizes that the promise of pornography to be fulfilling

was an empty lie. Though it promises intimacy, it fails to deliver the intimate connection God intended to take place between two human beings in a sexual relationship.

Though it promises intimacy, it fails to deliver the intimate connection God intended to take place between two human beings in a sexual relationship.

It is no secret that men are wired to be visual, which means that they can become easily aroused by what they see. Satan knows this is a fundamental way that men were created, and he uses this against us in ways that entangle the soul. When a man watches pornography, the images he sees don't just go away after he is finished watching it. Remember the illustration I gave earlier about how pornography is taken in through the senses but remains in the mind? This is why a man can have hundreds of images in a type of mental "Rolodex" that can pop up at any given moment throughout the day. The more porn he consumes, the more images become stored in that Rolodex. These images become the "imaginations" and "high thoughts" that 2 Corinthians 10:5 talks about. It is bad enough that Satan tries to bombard our minds with lustful thoughts even when we *don't* use pornography, but watching porn is like willingly handing the devil material to use against your mind at any given time. You are fueling a battle in your soul and giving him the exact equipment he needs to destroy you.

For the married man using porn, this Rolodex of images can begin to invade his sexual relationship with his wife. We have established that pornography destroys real intimacy in relationships because it replaces real human interaction with a false image. When a married man trains his flesh to become dependent on pornography for sexual fulfillment, his wife can start to lose her appeal to him. He becomes more invested in his "relationship" with the women in porn than he does in his marriage. The images he sees can begin to influence how he wants his wife to perform in their sexual relationship, and he begins to compare her with a two-dimensional image on a computer screen. He may even lose control of the frequency and number of "imaginations" that appear on the screen of his mind. This is another example of a soul being "poor." Remember, God's desire is that the mind, will, and emotions of Christians be healthy, whole, and regulated by the Word of God. That only happens when the soul is submitted to the will of God.

God's desire is that the mind, will,
and emotions of Christians be healthy, whole,
and regulated by the Word of God.

Getting Free from the Addiction of Fantasy Sex

The first step to getting free from pornography addiction and sexual fantasizing that results from the habit is to recognize that it is wrong. The Word of God is the standard that we must abide by when it comes to evaluating whether something is acceptable to God or not. It is also the only way to get out of whatever it is we are doing. Sexual immorality is a work of the flesh and will cause you to not inherit the kingdom of God (Galatians 5:19–21). There are scriptures that talk about how Christians are to keep themselves from sexual immorality (1 Corinthians 6:18–20). Ephesians 5:3 in the Amplified Bible says that immorality and all impurity should not even be named among Christian people. Make no mistake about it, pornography use is *not* okay.

I believe that most Christian men are generally aware that viewing pornography is wrong. Because the Holy Spirit lives inside every born-again man, there is a sense of conviction that indicates that viewing pornography is not consistent with the character of Christ that is within them. To the conscience that has been calloused by repeated sin, fear, abuse, and repeated exposure to sexually explicit material, pornography is something normal and just another thing to do. The person with a calloused conscience will either plunge into self-loathing, condemnation, and crushing shame or create his own standards that allow him to continue indulging in pornography without any conviction. In either case, the Word of God and the grace of God are still the path to freedom.

Unfortunately, the people who tend to suffer most are the people who are in relationships with men who are involved in sex addiction.

Unfortunately, the people who tend to suffer most are the people who are in relationships with men who are involved in sex addiction. Much of the pain is absorbed by the wives, families, and friends who are often destroyed by the effects of porn use in a man's life, but the Word of God offers hope to the man struggling in this area. Part of the acknowledgment that it is wrong involves confession. The reason confession is so powerful and necessary is that it goes past denial, justification, and rationalizing behavior and moves a man toward a proper understanding of his own brokenness and need for deliverance and wholeness. It refuses to celebrate sin and helps to reestablish fellowship with God and other people. Romans 10:10 says that confession establishes salvation, which is wholeness in every area of our lives. There is something powerful that takes place in the life of a man who not only confesses the sin of pornography to God but also confesses it to someone else. When we share our sin with trusted people in our lives, it forces the issue into the light. We can no longer hide our issues and try to deal with them alone. The key is to expose the issue with a repentant heart. Only then can true recovery and healing begin to take place.

When we share our sin with trusted people in our lives, it forces the issue into the light.

Keep in mind that there is a difference between feeling sorry about doing something, or getting caught, and actually repenting. Repenting involves a change of mind, a change of heart, and a change of direction. When you repent, you make a decision to turn away from what displeases God and go in the opposite direction. You begin to implement a plan of action that includes boundary setting and account-ability to others as you go through your process. You make concrete decisions and take concrete practi-cal actions to protect and maintain your decision to repent. You must get to the point of complete bro-kenness and readiness to submit this area of your life to the authority of God's Word, and then do what is necessary to walk it out.

You begin to implement a plan of action that includes boundary setting and accountability to others as you go through your process.

Confession is difficult for many men because it indicates personal moral failure. Men don't like to admit failure, because to them it is a sign of weak-ness, which challenges their ideas about masculin-ity and what it means to be a man. This is why it is going to be critical that you confess your sin to someone who can help play a role in the healing pro-cess and won't belittle or shame you. Allow the Holy Spirit to lead you to the person with whom you are to disclose this very delicate issue. The individual needs to be trustworthy, supportive, compassionate, and emotionally able to handle the information without cracking under the weight of it. Whoever you share with, understand that this is part of the process of deliverance.

I cannot stress enough the importance of accountability to the right people. Many men try to be accountable to their peers, but when it comes to breaking free from sexually driven addictions, you need an older, wiser, mature man of God who can serve as a mentor. Sometimes your friends and peers have the same struggles, and while they may be able to empathize with you, they are not always able to actually be a source of true accountability. A seasoned Christian man can impart wisdom and spiritual direction that your peers cannot. This is someone who has weathered the trials of life and has gone through the process of deliverance himself.

I cannot stress enough the importance of accountability to the right people.

One of the lies that the world tries to sell men is that having meaningful relationships with other men is not necessary or manly. Worldly thinking limits male relationships to bonding over sports and activities that objectify women. Anything outside of these two outlets is typically viewed as less masculine in some way. But God never intended for men to be isolated from each other outside of these two contexts. Too many men have too few close male friends whom they can really open up to. Their friendships only run as deep as the things they do together, but outside of that, there is not real transparency. Locating trusted male friends whom you can open up to allows for emotional needs to be met in a healthy way that does not involve acting out sexually. Don't feel restricted in your relationships with your brothers in Christ; you need them and they need you in order to grow.

---

*Too many men have too few close male friends
whom they can really open up to.*

Once you acknowledge the problem and confess it to someone, it is important to locate the root of the behavior. This basically means identifying why you act out the way you do. This is where the hard and often painful work of self-evaluation comes into play. This may mean revisiting childhood experiences or other issues that are a part of your personal history. In doing so, you can begin to identify patterns and life cycles that helped to shape your habits today.

The Holy Spirit is such a wonderful resource in the deliverance process. He is our Helper, and He searches our hearts. The Holy Spirit will bring to your remembrance the things that trigger a pattern of behavior even when you are not aware. He will show you the present emotional "triggers" that move you into a cycle of addictive behavior. He will even lead you to other men of God, counselors, and advisors who can assist. Invite God into the process and be open to receive what He reveals to you. Through the Word of God and the Holy Spirit, you can receive a new blueprint for manhood and masculinity that aligns with God's plan for your life.

The Holy Spirit is such a wonderful resource in the deliverance process.

The Word of God is, of course, the primary tool that you must use to retrain your thinking. More important than any other step to breaking addictive habits is the necessity of spending significant amounts of time in the Word daily, meditating and speaking the Scriptures. The more Word you plant in your heart, the more rapidly your progress will take place. When you read, study, meditate, and speak the Word of God over your life, you are planting new "seeds" in your heart, seeds that are guaranteed to bring forth life, purity, and the character of Christ. That Word will go down into your subconscious mind and begin rooting out the wrong thought patterns and beliefs that have been planted there through the lies of pornography. As you allow the Word of God to transform your thinking, you will find yourself conforming to the image of Christ from the inside out. Your thoughts, words, and desires will begin to change and you will eventually begin to see pornography for what it really is—a counterfeit form of intimacy that adds absolutely no spiritual value to your life whatsoever.

The more Word you plant in your heart, the more rapidly your progress will take place.

God loves you. He desires to have such a close relationship with you that you never feel the need to turn to anything outside His Word for fulfillment. He wants to heal you and bring wholeness to the areas of your life that are broken. Be courageous and resolute in your stand against addiction and other destructive behavior. Know that anything the devil has to offer you will only end in pain and heartache. Satan's goal is to steal, kill, and destroy your life; however, Jesus came to give you an abundant life that is free from moral conflict and the battles of the flesh that rage against your spirit. By choosing to walk in the Spirit, which is walking in the Word, you will find yourself walking right out of addiction and into a life of peace, joy, and fulfillment. Choose life and the freedom that is only found in Christ!

Be courageous and resolute in your stand against addiction and other destructive behavior.

10

THE STANDARD OF GRACE

Mark the perfect man, and behold the
upright: for the end of that man is peace.

—PSALM 37:37

Praise ye the LORD. Blessed is the man
that feareth the LORD, that delighteth
greatly in his commandments.
His seed shall be mighty upon earth:
the generation of the upright shall be blessed.
Wealth and riches shall be in his house:
and his righteousness endureth for ever.

—PSALM 112:1–3

So many Christians feel powerless and are unable to overcome their struggles because they do not realize that God has empowered them to be successful in every arena of their lives. This empowerment is actually God's grace, which enables us to live in a way that pleases Him and to serve acceptably. We tend to get hung up on our faults and flaws, which produces a sin-consciousness. Condemnation has a paralyzing effect on our progress, and it actually keeps us in a cycle of feeling inferior. The truth is that when we accept Jesus Christ as our Lord and Savior, we become the beneficiary of a new covenant that is governed by the grace of God. God wants this new standard to be etched on our souls and constantly in our minds. The standard of grace is the empowerment we need to be more than conquerors through Jesus Christ.

In order to understand this new standard for living the Christian life, it is important that we understand the difference between the old and the new covenants.

In order to understand this new standard for living the Christian life, it is important that we understand the difference between the old and the new covenants. One of the things that has been responsible for keeping so many Christians in bondage, where guilt and condemnation are concerned, is not having a correct understanding of the new covenant that has been implemented through the sacrifice of Jesus Christ. Many Christians maintain a sin-consciousness because they are trying to submit themselves to the Law rather than receive the liberty and freedom that comes from knowing that their sins have been forgiven through Jesus' shed blood. We are now living under the dispensation of grace, which means that we are not subject to the Law implemented by Moses. Knowing this is critical to living a successful Christian life.

When we talk about the "Law," we are talking about the guidelines that were put in place in the Old Testament pertaining to how God's people were supposed to live. The Law was implemented for the purpose of making mankind aware of its need for a Savior. Under the old covenant, God had a part and man had a part. Man's part was to offer sacrifices to God for the purpose of covering his sins, and God's part was to respond by blessing the sacrifice. This is why the Jews in the Old Testament repeatedly offered animal sacrifices to God. They had to because under the Law the only way to remain in right standing with God was to offer a burnt sacrifice to Him. However, one of the effects of the Law was that it bred sin-consciousness in the hearts and minds of people. Because they were not born again, they were subject to this sin-consciousness, and there was nothing they could do about it. They had their sins on their minds and the idea that they had to *do* something to eradicate them.

However, one of the effects of the Law was that it bred sin-consciousness in the hearts and minds of people.

Please understand, the Law was holy and good. But the problem with it was that no one could keep it perfectly. Although the sacrifices the Jews made to God allowed them to be blessed in spite of not keeping the Law, those sacrifices had to be performed over and over again. The truth is that God knew we needed a Savior, an ultimate sacrifice to perfectly fulfill the Law and make us righteous in His sight forever. This is why Jesus came to the earth. He became that ultimate sacrifice once and for all, throughout eternity. When we receive Him as our

Lord and Savior, we enter into a new covenant that is based on God's grace, not the Law, which requires us to *do* something to gain righteousness before God.

***The truth is that God knew we
needed a Savior***

Hebrews 8:6–13 paints a picture of this new covenant that we are part of as Christians:

But now hath he obtained a more excellent ministry, by how much also he is the mediator of a better covenant, which was established upon better promises. For if that first covenant had been faultless, then should no place have been sought for the second. For finding fault with them, he saith, Behold, the days come, saith the Lord, when I will make a new covenant with the house of Israel and with the house of Judah: Not according to the covenant that I made with their fathers in the day when I took them by the hand to lead them out of the land of Egypt; because they continued not in my covenant, and I regarded them not, saith the Lord. For this is the covenant that I will make with the house of Israel after those days, saith the Lord; I will put my laws in their

hearts: and I will be to them a God and they
shall be to me a people...For I will be merci-
ful to their unrighteousness, and their sins and
their iniquities will I remember no more. In that
he saith, A new covenant, he hath made the first
old. Now that which decayeth and waxeth old is
ready to vanish away.

He has put His Spirit in our hearts, enabling
us to have a personal relationship with
Him through Jesus Christ.

For the born-again Believer today, there is a new
covenant and, consequently, a new spiritual reality
for us to partake of, as evidenced by this Hebrews
passage. Because we cannot keep the Law in its
entirety, God has made a new agreement with us in
which He has put His Spirit in our hearts, enabling
us to have a personal relationship with Him through
Jesus Christ. With the Holy Spirit within us, we
become aware of God's requirements, and God personally teaches us about who He is on an intimate
level. He promises to be merciful to us and completely forget about our sins and iniquities! In this
new covenant, God's part is to release the Blessing
into our lives through Jesus Christ, who is our High

Priest, and our part is to simply believe, receive, and give Him thanks for what He has done for us. It is a covenant agreement that is based on our faith in Jesus and not our own efforts to become righteous in God's sight.

Understanding the covenant of grace enables us to live free from sin-consciousness.

Understanding the covenant of grace enables us to live free from sin-consciousness, which is a huge problem in many Christians' lives. When they miss the mark, they have the nagging feeling that God is angry with them. Then they do it again and feel even worse. Having a Law-based consciousness will keep you in a position of constantly trying to get right with God through your own good works, which completely disregards the grace of God that actually *equips* you to live above sin. Knowing that God does not remember our sins when we confess them, turn away from them, and accept Jesus into our hearts, allows us to walk through life free from condemnation when we make mistakes. The blood of Jesus is continually working to cleanse us as we walk in the light of God's Word that we know. We must believe in God's love for us and know that He never goes back on His promises. If He has said that we are for-given, then we are forgiven. Receive the freedom that comes from understanding the new covenant!

Strength in the Midst of Weakness

The beauty of Christianity is that once you become born again God literally empowers you with the abil-ity to obey the Word of God. Titus 2:12 says that the grace of God trains us to reject and renounce ungodli-ness and worldly desires, and to live upright lives in the midst of a fallen world. You possess grace in your re-created spirit, and that grace is what enables you to live a successful Christian life and fulfill the will of God. You simply have to access the grace of God by faith.

> *The beauty of Christianity is that once you become born again God literally empowers you with the ability to obey the Word of God.*

Grace is not only receiving unmerited favor from God, but it is also an empowerment for supernatural results. There is nothing impossible for you because of the grace of God. Whatever you cannot do in your natural ability can be done through God's ability or grace. This is particularly important for men, because we tend to move in the direction of self-effort and want to "make it happen." However, part of being a man of faith is trusting in God's grace more than you do your own abilities. Your degrees, career, and intellect cannot and will never be able to get the job done in and of themselves. Can God use those things as part of His kingdom strategy in your life? Of course He can! However, we have to begin to rely on the grace of God as our source of empowerment.

However, part of being a man of faith is trusting in God's grace more than you do your own abilities.

The more you meditate on the grace of God and its reality in your life by finding out what the Word has to say about it, the more your faith in God's grace will grow. Faith in the grace of God is what connects you to it. This frees you from trying to accomplish things in your own ability and puts the onus on God to get the job done. You simply walk in the reality of His grace and do whatever He tells you to do.

Second Corinthians 12:9 says something that really embodies how grace works in our lives, especially when we are spiritually weak. In this scripture, the Apostle Paul was reflecting on a particular weakness that he was dealing with, and he records what God spoke to him about it: "And he said unto me, My grace is sufficient for thee: for my strength is made perfect in weakness. Most gladly therefore will I rather glory in my infirmities, that the power of Christ may rest upon me."

The beauty of grace is that it works best when you are weak. God says that His grace is all you need when you are dealing with personal battles, trials, or weaknesses of your flesh. Don't try to manage those things in your own strength; you will fail every time. Instead, release your faith in God's grace by declaring, "When I am weak, God's grace strengthens me. I am empowered to overcome because of His ability working in and through me, not my own ability." You will be amazed at how your faith in God's grace will soar when you make this kind of confession.

The beauty of grace is that it works best when you are weak.

I can remember a time when our ministry had a real financial need where our television broadcast was concerned. There was a bill that needed to be paid, and I had no idea where the money would come from. I had to take some time to get before God on my own and really tap into my faith in His grace. There was absolutely nothing I could do in my own ability or through my own natural resources to meet the need, and the bill had to be paid in order to stay on television. I cast my care on God that day and made a decision to stand on His Word and believe God, no matter what. By releasing my faith in God's provision, I connected to His provision, and He met the need. That was the grace of God in operation.

I had to take some time to get before God on my own and really tap into my faith in His grace.

Withdrawing Spiritual Resources

Many times we are so focused on trying to get something to happen that we fail to realize that what we need already resides on the inside of us. Healing, financial prosperity, deliverance, and every spiritual blessing we need to be victorious in life, in our relationships, and in our marriages is *already* within us. So how do we pull those resources out of the spiritual realm so we can see them manifest in our everyday lives?

There are several ways we can tap into the grace necessary to see manifestation in our lives:

1. Through Renewing Your Mind

The Bible says in Romans 12:1, 2 that we are to renew our minds so that our thinking is not conformed to the world's way of doing things. Self-effort is the world's way of getting things done. Those who rely on self-effort depend on the intellect and other abilities outside of God. Many times we may try to come up with solutions to our problems or ways to handle things that are not based on the Word of God but on "self." This is not the way to access grace. We have to spend time in the Word, meditating on the Scriptures until they become more real to us than anything else. Our own self-effort has to take a backseat to the ability of God. And why wouldn't you want it to? Grace makes things easier for us because we can lean on God totally and completely. It is Him working through us that makes things happen. Renewing your mind is the key to this.

We have to spend time in the Word.

2. By Using Your Faith

Faith is the access key to God's grace. Without faith, we cannot get in contact with God's power. Faith connects us to the supernatural realm. The Word of God is the source of the faith we need to see grace work in our lives. So, the more of the Word we read, meditate, and take into our spirits, the more faith we will have. And the more faith we have, the more of the supernatural we will experience.

Faith connects us to the supernatural realm.

---

3. By Acknowledging the Supernatural Resources We Have within Our Spirits

Philemon 1:6 says, "That the communication of thy faith may become effectual by the acknowledging of every good thing which is in you in Christ Jesus." When we acknowledge the grace we have within us, we are not just quoting statements. Instead, we are admitting the power that is within us—that it is real. We have the power of might, healing, and abundance, and God's very nature within us. However, the grace within us lies dormant until we use our faith to transfer that grace into the natural realm.

When we believe God's Word instead of what we see in the natural realm, we are believing with our hearts. If we acknowledge Him in all our ways, He will give us the direction we need. This is a manifestation of grace. It starts with recognizing what we possess inside of us.

If we acknowledge Him in all our ways,
He will give us the direction we need.

---

4. By Praying in Tongues

Praying in tongues is another way to release the grace of God and withdraw spiritual resources from within us. When you pray in the Spirit, you renew your strength, pray for unknown things, allow the Spirit of God to intercede for and through you, draw out spiritual wisdom, and stir up the gifts of the Spirit. This is the most effective way to pray the perfect will of God and release the supernatural into every area of your life.

5. By Operating in the Fear of the Lord

To "fear the Lord" simply means to respect and honor Him. It is not being afraid of God in the sense of being frightened, but it is to hold His Word in the highest regard. When you make the Word of God your final authority, the power of God can be released to get involved in your situations and circumstances. The grace of God that is operating in your life is connected to the fear of the Lord. God is pleased when we obey Him.

The grace of God is a free gift that was imparted to us at the moment of salvation.

You have an advocate with the Father—Jesus Christ—and you have His ability in your re-created spirit. The grace of God is a free gift that was imparted to us at the moment of salvation. What kind of father would give his children instructions and not give them the tools they need to carry those instructions out? Certainly not our heavenly Father! He loves us so much that not only did He give us fail-safe guidelines by which to live that will put us in a position to live an abundant life, but He also gave us His very own ability! We possess all we need to experience ultimate victory as Christians in this world. Nothing is impossible for the person who accesses grace by faith. Receive it and lay hold of the success and victory that rightfully belong to you!

11

CONFESSIONS FOR MEN

And it shall come to pass in the last days, saith God, I will pour out of my Spirit upon all flesh: and your sons and your daughters shall prophesy, and your young men shall see visions, and your old men shall dream dreams...

—ACTS 2:17

I am a man of honor, integrity, and character.

I am a man of love. God loves me, and His love is shed abroad in my heart by the Holy Spirit. I walk in love and forgive those who have hurt me or offended me.

I am God's beloved. He loves and accepts me unconditionally.

I model my life after Jesus Christ. He is my example of manhood.

I renew my mind with the Word of God, and I do not conform to the world's way of thinking. By renewing my mind, I am able to prove what is the acceptable and perfect will of God for my life.

I am a spirit, I possess a soul, and I live in a physical body. My body is the temple of the Holy Spirit, and my mind, will, and emotions are subject to the Word of God. I live a Spirit-led life, not a flesh-led life.

I gain my sense of identity from Christ. I am in Him, and He is in me. I reign in life by Christ and I have victory in Him.

I am the righteousness of God in Christ, and I have liberty in Him. I have been blessed with all spiritual blessings in Christ Jesus.

I reject selfishness and embrace a life of servanthood as I follow Christ's example. As I serve others in the spirit of love, I position myself to be a godly leader in my household, on my job, and in ministry.

God has not given me a spirit of fear, but power, love, and a sound mind. I do not walk in fear; I walk in faith.

I have boldness to stand before the Father without a sense of guilt, inferiority, or condemnation.

The grace of God is operating in my life, empowering me to live in a way that pleases God and to obey His Word.

I am equipped by grace to fulfill the will of God for my life.

I tread upon serpents and scorpions, and I exercise righteous authority over all the power of the enemy. Nothing shall by any means hurt me. I am skilled in the Word of righteousness, and I call things that be not as though they were. I will not fear what man or spirit can do to me because no weapon formed against me shall prosper. Any tongue that rises against me in judgment shall be condemned.

I rely on the grace of God to accomplish what I cannot accomplish in my own ability. I let go of self-effort and trust God wholeheartedly.

My righteousness in not based on my good works, but it is based on what Jesus has done for me. I am in right standing with God.

I renounce all pride, arrogance, ego, disobedience, and rebellion in the name of Jesus.

I am a man of love, and my character reflects the fruit of the Spirit.

God loves me. I am His beloved, and God is for me.

I rest in Jesus' finished work by faith.

Satan has no power over me. I renew my mind with God's Word and my soul comes into alignment with my born-again spirit.

I renounce all ungodly thought patterns and belief systems in the name of Jesus. I put on the mind of Christ.

My faith grows exceedingly. I am a man of faith.

I speak words of faith and refuse to speak in a way that goes against the Word of God.

My words reflect what is in my heart, and my heart is full of the Word of God.

I am increasing in the knowledge of God, and I am strengthened with all might according to His glorious power.

I know my purpose in life, and I am executing it through and by the grace of God. Confusion is not a part of my life. I hear the Lord's voice clearly and follow His instructions.

I keep my mind focused on God, and He keeps me in perfect peace. My mind is free from agitating passions and moral conflicts because I continually meditate on the Word of God.

I value the relationships in my life, and I seek out relationships that foster my spiritual growth.

I am accountable to God and maintain an awareness of His presence at all times.

I meditate on the Word of God and make my way prosperous in life.

I am a recipient of God's favor in every area of my life.

God is my strength in the midst of the storms of life. He is a very present help in the midst of trouble.

I look into the mirror of God's Word, and there I find my true identity. The Word reflects back to me the way God sees me and, therefore, the way I see myself.

I commune with God in prayer daily and allow my time with Him to fulfill my needs for spiritual intimacy.

God's healing is available to me. I am healed and made whole in every area of my life, physically, spiritually, emotionally, and mentally.

I let go of my past and press into the future God has for me. His plan for my life is perfect and was established before the foundations of the world.

When I need wisdom, I ask God for it, and He liberally gives it to me. Jesus is my wisdom, righteousness, and sanctification.

I can do all things through Christ, who strengthens me.

I am greatly blessed, highly favored, and deeply loved.

ABOUT THE AUTHOR

Dr. Creflo Dollar is the founder and senior pastor of World Changers Church International (WCCI) in College Park, Georgia; World Changers Church–New York; and satellite churches like World Changers Church–Houston, Los Angeles, and Norcoss. His award-winning *Changing Your World* broadcast reaches nearly one billion homes around the world. Dr. Dollar is the publisher of *Change*, an online magazine featuring inspiring, challenging, and life-changing articles that deal with everyday life issues, and *The Max*, a resource newsletter for ministry leaders. A much-sought-after conference speaker, Dr. Dollar has books, CDs, audiotapes, and videotapes in worldwide distribution. He is the author of *The Holy Spirit, Your Financial Advisor, 8 Steps to Create the Life You Want, Winning In Troubled Times*, and

The Divine Order of Faith, which has been added to the curricula of Christian colleges across the United States. He and his wife, Taffi, have five children and live in Atlanta, Georgia. You can visit Creflo Dollar Ministries at www.creflodollarministries.org.